ENTERTAINMENT TECHNOLOGY PRESS

In taking advantage of the latest in 'print on demand' digital printing techniques, Entertainment Technology Press is approaching book publishing in a very different way. By establishing a wide range of highly specific technical books that can be kept up-to-date in a continuing publishing process, our plan is to cover the entertainment technology sector with a wide range of individual titles.

As will be seen by examining the back cover of this book, the ETP list is divided into various categories so as to allow sufficient room for generic growth and development of each title. To ensure the quality of the books and the success of the project the publishers are building up a team of authors who are practising in and well-respected by the industry. As specialists within a particular field of activity it is anticipated that each author will stay closely involved with 'their' title or titles for an extended period.

All Entertainment Technology Press titles have a dedicated area on the publisher's own website at www.etnow.com where latest information and up-dates can be accessed by purchasers of the books concerned. This additional service is included within the purchase price of all titles.

Readers and prospective authors are invited to submit any ideas and comments they may have on the Entertainment Technology Press series to the Series Editor either by post to the address below or by email to editor@etnow.com

D1440036

This i

www.rosco.com

STAGE LIGHTING FOR THEATRE DESIGNERS

Nigel Morgan

TECHNOLOGY PRESS

Application and Techniques Series

cover photograph: *A **Midsummer Night's Dream***, The Sherman Theatre, Cardiff, 1994

STAGE LIGHTING FOR THEATRE DESIGNERS

Nigel Morgan

Entertainment Technology Press

Stage Lighting for Theatre Designers

© Nigel Morgan

First published 1995 by The Herbert Press Ltd.
This edition published June 2003 by
Entertainment Technology Press Ltd
The Studio, High Green, Great Shelford, Cambridge, CB2 5EG
Internet: www.etnow.com

ISBN 1 904031 19 6

A title within the
Entertainment Technology Press Application and Techniques Series
Series editor: John Offord

CODE / SLTD001

CONTENTS

ACKNOWLEDGEMENTS

The author acknowledges the help received from various manufacturers through provision of illustrations, and Jackie Staines of Entertainment Technology Press for her assistance in collation of photographic material.

FOREWORD

I'm very pleased to write the foreword to this book by Dr. Nigel Morgan. As he says, you cannot see light until it hits something so writing about lighting is not easy. Making rules about lighting is even more difficult. Nigel gives us a practical approach to solving the problems.

What excites me about lighting design is that it combines art with science. The lighting designer has to convert ideas into light using a technical medium. It also combines creativity with practicality, and imagination with reality. The designer needs to illuminate as well as create mood and atmosphere, describe locations, time of day, or respond to particular emotions expressed in the performance, as well as helping to tell the story and punctuate the piece.

In revisiting this book since it was first published it is interesting to reflect on how things have moved on. Technology has taken big strides in the way we can use light. The programming of cues and effects has become more complex and can take longer. To a certain extent we can visualise lighting on computers and pre-programme focus positions for moving lights. The place of the lighting designer as a key player in the creative team is assured. It is quite normal for the lighting designer to be contracted at the same time as the stage designer. I believe that expectations of what the lighting designer can produce and the amount of time the designer is required have increased far more than the associated financial remuneration.

Some things haven't changed. There can be a number of scary moments in the lighting process, like having to talk about lighting at the early design stage long before the piece gets into rehearsal and the lights are focused. The conversations that take place between the key members of the creative team at this stage are vital. The lighting designer needs to absorb what the writer is saying in the script as well as meeting with the writer, the director, designers, and choreographer. Of course, it is more difficult to talk about what one might do with the light at this stage than it is to show a set or costume design. To work well and comfortably there needs to be a high level of support, trust and confidence between the creative team.

Armed with information, ideas and hopefully inspiration the lighting designer faces the next scary stage; to transform a blank piece of paper into a lighting rig that is going to meet all the needs of the production as well as work within the resource restraints of equipment, people and budget. Creating the rig can be fun, but rest assured if you have 24 channels you will want 25, and if you have 500 lights you will want 501! I don't think it gets easier when the rig gets bigger.

We don't really get to prove ourselves until the production moves onto the stage. So at the moment when you create your first lighting state and perhaps nervously ask the director: "Did you mean something like this?" you can find that you are surrounded by other members of the creative and technical team, not to mention producers too. To create the lighting the designer is thrust into a world where the design can only be realised in the rather public forum of the stage with the added pressure of restricted time to achieve the results. Sometimes I think people forget that the creation of lighting is a gradual process and it takes time and some rehearsals to refine and develop it. The lighting design can only be appreciated when it is combined with all the other elements of set, costume, projections, sound, music, actors, dancers and singers in performance.

This book examines the creative and practical stages of lighting design through to performance. It looks at both the hardware and the technical means that we use to create lighting. It shows a way of analyzing the artistic needs of the production. It addresses electrical safety and the need to work within the resources available.

In writing this book Nigel Morgan combines his practical background both as a technician and lighting designer with his extensive experience as a teacher of lighting and theatre skills to find a creative, logical and constructive route through the lighting process.

I am sure that this book will enhance and develop the understanding of anyone involved in the creative process of lighting. I hope you enjoy the book and learn something too. I certainly did.

Mark Jonathan
Head of Lighting
Royal National Theatre, London
February 1995 and May 2003

INTRODUCTION

It gives me great pleasure to introduce the second edition of my book, *Stage Lighting for Theatre Designers*. When updating the text, pictures and diagrams, and reflecting back on the changes that have taken place in lighting since the first edition was written in 1994, I was reminded of how little the process of design and production has changed. Where changes have occurred, they have been in technological developments. The two most important have been new generations of conventional lanterns of greater optical and energy efficiency, and digital control now being fully established in the profession. With the cost of entry into this level of technology becoming increasingly affordable, many young people at school can learn lighting with high quality lanterns and memory controls. Similarly, computer aided design packages have tumbled in price, and moving lights, scrollers and other gizmos seem to be commonplace now in all areas of the performance business. Yet none of these developments have changed the way we think about lighting, or indeed practice lighting. And it is these processes that this book sets out to describe.

Theatrical performance styles have changed greatly over the centuries, with the most dramatic and frequent changes occurring during the last hundred years. As man's vision of the role of theatre in society has changed, so too has stage design, harnessing new technologies in harmony with new styles of writing and new ways of interpreting text. Electric light was first introduced to the theatre in 1881. Stage designers soon found this new medium potent, to become pivotal to the shaping of the stage picture in the twentieth century. Technological developments since 1970 have meant that lighting has become a sophisticated design tool, and many of today's high profile events and performances are completely dependent on lighting for presence, effect, style and spectacle.

In 1994 I wrote of the problems that lighting designers could have in being accepted into the creative team. Fortunately those days are now generally behind us. Projects such as the Millennium Dome and the presentation of leading rock and music artists have brought lighting design into the mind of the general public, and the status of those who command it is now much higher. The 'Art' theatres have benefited from this too, with cheaper, better quality equipment now available for rental, and a more advanced visual dictionary in the domain for directors and designers to draw on for inspiration. There is now a degree programme in Lighting Design in the UK, and this has contributed to the lighting designer being a respected creative artist, with pay and conditions improving.

For the work of the lighting designer really is crucial to the success of a performance. Once the concept of a play has been decided by the director and creative team (which includes the lighting designer), it is the lighting designer's job to interpret the concept through the medium of light and produce a finished lighting scheme, on schedule, within the resources available, and achieving the highest visual aesthetic and ambition possible. In order to achieve this, I believe that a lighting designer requires three particular attributes: a detailed, intimate understanding and an imagination of how lighting can be used creatively in a play; the technical skills to translate ideas into lighting schemes; and the managerial ability and communications skills to organise him- or herself and others. I think that these attributes are well summed up by an analogy: the lighting designer must combine an artist's imagination and powers of observation with an engineer's functionalism and understanding of materials with an architect's project management skills.

This book's primary aim is to help the emerging theatre lighting designer acquire more knowledge of and insight into how light can be used in a theatre production. It should also be useful for other theatre personnel, such as the director who may wish to advance their ideas of the contribution lighting can make to the theatre. Clearly no book is a substitute for practical hands-on experience, but this book is both a springboard and a thorough guide to all the processes involved.

Clearly, the best starting point for any lighting designer is an understanding of the physical behaviour of light and how it affects our vision. Next you need knowledge of what lighting can bring to a production. This comes partly from study, partly from experience of theatre, but partly also from observing life. In the same way that an actor makes character studies, so too the lighting designer must build up an image bank of the effect lighting has on our lives, and must draw on recollections of different lighting conditions in different situations. The image bank might include, for example: the look of a dull, wet, cold woodland; the sunlight of a late afternoon in Tuscany; or an intimidating industrial setting at night time – three very different evocative lighting situations; or equally, less realistic or emotional conditions, such as threat, anger, despair or love.

Anyone with an interest in theatre, a keen sense of observation and a fertile imagination, beginner or otherwise, can have sound ideas for theatre lighting. There are sometimes wrong answers to the problems posed by staging of a play, but very often it is a question of artistic taste, judgement and appreciation, and even a beginner can have an instinctive feel for what is right.

Without the equipment no lighting ideas can be realised. So you will need a thorough knowledge of the available equipment. In an ideal world, a lighting designer would like to use any of the wide range of equipment on the market to achieve the desired effect. Naturally, of course, there are constraints, usually those of budget, time and space. Experience shows how to overcome such difficulties, but this book also provides some suggestions.

The next step is to discover how to break a play down into manageable segments and how to set about lighting each of those segments. Then comes learning how to make the best of the equipment and achieve a 'look' through clever control of the variables.

The lighting designer will also have to be comfortable being lead by a director, being an equal member of a creative team, and leading a team of electricians and crew. Each requires different interpersonal skills, and these can be severely tested under the pressures of a production period. This book will help you develop your role within a production team.

And so, from conception to realisation. The play's director gathers the creative team together. Each member works separately and as a team to realise the design concept in his or her medium so that hopefully, on opening night, all the elements come together to produce a satisfying interpretation of the play.

To show how this can be achieved in practice, I use a theoretical production of Shakespeare's *A Midsummer Night's Dream* to illustrate the processes of lighting. I also offer three 'new plays' as case studies that illustrate contrasting ways in which I have used light in professional situations.

A reading list is included that details my personal choice of the six 'must have' books on lighting, and the addresses of the key UK organisations for further information.

The design of stage lighting is a complex process requiring a knowledge of many disparate pieces of information almost from the work go. Thus it is sometimes inevitable that I mention a point before there has been a chance to explain it in context. For ease of reading I have tried to keep cross-references to a minimum, but there are some instances where this is unavoidable.

So what will happen in the next ten years? I confidently predict that any book written in 2013 will have sections on: Light Emitting Diode (LED) lanterns; converting your domestic PC into a control desk; and details of how projected images have increased in sophistication, brightness and accessibility. But it is my guess that the processes described here will remain universal – and that there will still be small venues with traditional facilities: manual control, 24 or less ways of dimming, Patt. 23s and 123s amongst the lantern stock; and that, as now, these venues will be the proving ground for the next generation of lighting designers.

1 LIGHT AND PERFORMANCE

Lighting is an essential component in today's theatre if only to make the actors visible in the darkened indoor space. But the role of lighting in the theatre is far more sophisticated than this; otherwise why not simply have floodlight-style illumination as at sports events?

As will be seen, lighting has two main functions. First, it can underpin the performance style of a play. Second, and often without the audience realising, it can assist with the storytelling to the point where it is helping direct the audience where to look and is controlling the emotional response. You may think these two functions are separate, but in a play where the lighting has been well designed, they are, in fact, inseparable.

Performance styles and lighting conventions

Let us look at style first. Certain types or genres of theatre have evolved their own particular lighting styles. These genres include: drama, dance, opera, musical, ballet, rock concert, etc. The seasoned theatre-goer will be aware of very different lighting styles for each of these performance forms.

Light contributes differently to each genre. In drama it is mainly used to create environments for the actor to inhabit that are closely related to reality. In modern dance light is used to create mood, texture and rhythm that reacts with and against the performer and the score. This requires a style of light that also enhances the body, shape and form, whereas drama - primarily requiring the actors' faces to be visible – there is an old saying, that if the actor cannot be seen, he cannot be heard. It would be most odd to light a rock band in the style of a Shakespearian tragedy, and vice versa. Thus a musical requires a different lighting style from a drama. For example, during a piece of dialogue a scene in a musical might be lit quite realistically as in a drama but as soon as a character on stage bursts into song, it is common for the singer to be lit by a follow spot – a pool of light that follows the performer's moves. Immediately the sense of realism is gone and a different more fantastic style emerges. Similarly, a piece of comedy dialogue in a musical will probably be lit with lanterns in similar positions and combinations to those in a comedy drama, but the musical genre often allows more exaggeration in the lighting, and richer coloured gels can be used (see Chapter 5).

Conventions like these are unique to certain genres, but some conventions are shared with other theatre forms. Common to all dialogue genres is the convention that comedy is lit brightly and tragedy broodily. Another shared convention, and one which not even regular theatre-goers may be consciously aware of, is that used at the very beginning of a show when the house lights fade gently over a space of five to seven seconds. This reassures the audience. They know that there will be nothing too confrontational ahead. But if a lighting designer chooses to snap out the houselights suddenly, it can be to warn the audience that there are some major emotional challenges on the way. It is therefore important for you as lighting designer to have a good understanding of different performance genres, styles and conventions when creating your own design.

Dramatic style

As well as the different theatre genres and the conventions that go with them, a lighting designer must understand the different styles of theatre staging – dramatic styles such as realism, naturalism, expressionism and so on that set the mood and atmosphere of a play. When a director is working in one of these styles, it is important for the lighting designer to reflect this in the style of lighting chosen.

Although similar style terminology can be applied to lighting styles, stage lighting can create a style that is anything from a realistic feel — a recreation of real-life conditions, to an unrealistic feel — a creation of abstract lighting conditions that goes against real-life experience.

If most plays are best served by lighting that creates a believable environment for the actor, then it is a matter of judgement how realistic or abstracted this will be. This judgement will be informed in part by what issues the play addresses, the historical period to which it belongs and the dramatic structure of the text. Most of all it is informed by the words the actors speak and the manner in which they are directed.

Storytelling

In all good storytelling, the audience has to feel involved in the action. The style of lighting plays its part in the storytelling too. In a play set in the nineteenth century, the recreation of gas-style lighting may help the audience to feel that they are in that period. Or the lighting might suggest a time of day or a season.

Lighting also helps with the storytelling by guiding the audience through the story, focusing on characters or details that are relevant at any given point.

Our eyes are most at ease when they can focus on one thing and relax their peripheral vision. In artificial lighting conditions we naturally look at the brightest object in our field of vision and only half-focus on the rest. So, for instance, when watching a film, we are most comfortable when the room is darkened and the screen is the brightest object we see.

And so it is in the theatre. The lighting designer can make the audience focus on, for example, the actor who is speaking. This can be simply achieved by focusing the brightest light on that actor. The other stage lighting then needs to taper away from the acting area so that the top and extreme side edges of the set are barely lit. Add to this a blacked-out auditorium, and the whole effect of the lighting is to help us keep our attention focused. We can now see tiny details of the object we are focusing on too. Even from the rear of the auditorium we can comfortably focus on the eyes of the actor who is speaking. If this actor speaks for some time, our focus becomes even more concentrated and intense while our awareness of the rest of the stage — our field of peripheral vision — narrows. A lighting designer can intensify this effect by 'closing down' the lighting around the actor, a subtle effect that is quite common practice.

Our awareness of the rest of the stage remains limited until something happens to disturb our concentration. This may be another actor starting to speak or move, in which case he becomes the one we need to look at. Or it may be that a new actor is about to enter, in which case it may be appropriate for the lighting designer to ask for lighting levels to be raised on one side of the stage, to draw the audience's attention to that area.

So it is that lighting has the ability to control a moment and prepare the audience for the next, and it can do this throughout the play. But perhaps the most important role that lighting can play is in helping the audience to follow or track the way the characters on stage are feeling. By helping to convey a character's mood, lighting can be one of the most powerful technical tools at the disposal of the director and, with its ability to be constantly changing, is unique among all the design elements of the theatre. As a character progresses through a play or as an actor progresses through a speech, the lighting can subtly shift to reflect the emotional changes that are occurring.

This can be done in several ways. Perhaps the most obvious is through the association that colour tones have with emotional feelings, an association that the theatre lighting designer can harness to good effect. For instance, we usually consider sunsets as romantic, not least because of the warm orange-red light. So too candlelight, which has the added advantage of low-intensity light giving a feeling of extra intimacy. Cool blue morning light is associated with freshness, while moonlight often goes hand in hand with intrigue. Warm tones such as straw colour and pinks can suggest happiness whereas cool tones like steel blue may reflect melancholy.

These straw and steel-blue tints, being close to the colours of natural light, are the most important and useful to the lighting designer. Switching or cross fading between the two can effectively follow a character's mood swing. So a change of lighting from a warm pink, through neutral white or pale lavender to cool blue can reflect a character's mood changing from happy to sad, calm to angry, or rational to irrational.

Colour is not the only way to track the emotions being conveyed on stage. A lighting designer can also use brightness and contrast. A bright, even, soft lighting on the face can indicate happiness. Reduce this until the actor is lit by a single spotlight, half in light, half in shadow, and an impression of sadness is conveyed. An actor may be seen in silhouette against a lit background. This emphasizes the shape of the actor's body rather than the face, suggesting his physical power rather than the verbal communication that comes from emphasizing the face.

Of course these devices will only be convincing if the text demands it and if the actor can realise the emotional shifts in the performance. In other words, a lighting designer can provide an actor's outer light but not his inner light.

General points about lighting

We have seen how lighting can help to underpin the production style of a play, and how it can help with the storytelling and with following the emotional shifts in the play. But just because the mood on stage changes, it does not necessarily mean that the lighting has to respond. The style in which a play is being performed – and sometimes the style of the stage set – will help to determine this. For instance, if the set is minimal, the lighting may become a major ingredient in the performance and many different changes of lighting may be appropriate. In contrast to this a highly detailed set may require little other than a few lighting changes to set the appropriate mood.

Whatever the style of the set, when you are formulating a design scheme, it pays to remember that not every play is a lighting epic requiring vast banks of lights and frequent light changes. Some plays clearly have more potential for lighting than others. A heavy Elizabethan tragedy such as *Macbeth* has tremendous possibilities for its lighting effects. Just flick through a design yearbook to see the range of staging styles a play such as this has been set in. By contrast, an Ibsen play probably has fewer desirable staging solutions and would almost certainly look best with natural-looking lighting and few lighting changes.

Thus lighting is equally important in all types of play, but you should choose it carefully. A play lit all through with just one look, or lighting state, and without any changes or cues may be far more relevant and powerful than one where the light changes every time an actor blinks. It may be fun to have lots of dramatic changes in your lighting, but be sure that the lighting is relevant and appropriate. There are few occasions where self-indulgence is justifiable.

Whatever the style of play, at the end of the day it is important to have a clear idea of your objectives. Establish clear, achievable targets and go for quality rather than quantity. It is far better to have a clear basic scheme that is executed to a high standard than to attempt a more ambitious one that is ragged due to lack of time or shortage of equipment. Insufficient production time is perhaps one of the greatest challenges you are likely to meet, and it is a true test of your skill to be able to scale your ideas to suit the circumstances. Arguably the best lighting design is that which has a carefully chosen style perfectly integrated with the staging, direction and performance, while working within the resources of the production.

2 ANALYSING LIGHT

How light travels

Light travels from the sun in parallel, invisible rays. Once the rays are generated they continue to travel until they hit an object in their path. When this happens, it is the light reflected by that object that enables us to see the object. In other words, we don't see light as it travels from the sun: we only see the object that interrupts the light. Similarly in the theatre. Light, once generated by a theatre lamp, will continue to travel until it hits an object and will then make that object visible.

In planning stage lighting it is important to remember that whereas light from the sun arrives on earth in parallel beams (the sun is so far away that the divergence of its beams is negligible), stage lighting instruments can only deliver diverging beams of light. Light will spread away from the lantern even when the lenses are set to narrow focus. The result is that the light's intensity reduces the farther away one goes from the lantern, so an actor standing 2 metres (6½feet) from a light source will look much brighter than one standing 4 metres (13 feet) from the same source. This fact makes it almost impossible to recreate the feeling of completely natural parallel beam sunlight using stage lighting equipment. While real daytime lighting is provided by one large light source in the sky – the sun – the stage has to be lit by many lanterns to achieve a similar lighting effect.

The effect of any light, whether it is the sun, a candle, or a theatre lantern, can be assessed in terms of its position, intensity, diffusion, contrast, texture and colour.

Position of the light source

The position of the sun in the sky has a dramatic effect on how we see things. There is constant change as the earth spins. A low dawn or dusk sunlight will light trees and buildings in a totally different way from high midday light. Light at dawn tends to be cool and crisp; at dusk, warm and lush. Whereas midday light can flatter objects by casting their shadows directly beneath them, low sun at the beginning and end of the day can make objects look bigger, more three-dimensional; perhaps, with long side shadows, more grotesque. You might notice how sunlight hitting a brick wall straight on will give it a flat two-dimensional appearance: if the sunlight were to skim the same wall from a low angle, the nooks and crannies in the bricks and mortar would be revealed, exaggerating the wall's three-dimensional qualities. So it is most important for the lighting designer to understand the different effects that the position of a light source creates, particularly as most lighting compositions involve the use of multi-position sources.

Intensity of the light source

All light sources have an intensity or brightness. The intensity of sunlight will depend on the time of day, the season of the year and the geographical location. You will no doubt have noticed the intensity of summer sunlight in the Mediterranean when the sun is at its height in the midday sky compared with sunlight in northern countries at the same time of day and year.

The intensity of light can be measured either subjectively by comparing one light to another, or accurately with a light meter. The unit of measurement used is a Lux. In many professions where lighting intensity levels have to be fixed to a certain predetermined level – such as film-making, television and architecture – the lighting designer will always measure the intensity of light with a meter. Film and video tape both require certain light intensity levels to record images accurately, while an architectural lighting designer must design buildings and rooms to be bright enough for the function they are to fulfil.

On stage, things are different, as there are no regulations. There, intensity of light is one of the most complex parameters to regulate. Lighting designers do not measure intensity using a meter, but simply by eye, comparing one lantern's output to another's, or one lighting state to another. Because the intensity is judged by eye, the tricks played by the eye come into the equation.

The iris is constantly opening and closing to regulate the amount of light let in. On a bright day it will close to reduce the light let in and to prevent a person from being dazzled, while at night it will open to allow in more light. While the eye can cope with enormous changes in intensity, it does need time to adapt if discomfort is to be avoided. Flash a torch into your eyes at night and you will see how this works.

The lighting designer can make use of this fact. Strike a match in daylight and the amount of light it emits is insignificant. But at night it can fill a small room. Therefore, after a blackout on stage, a scene at a very low light level will look quite bright for a time, while a dark scene following a bright one will look darker than it really is until the eye adjusts.

Light intensity is also affected by the colour of the surface that the light strikes. More power is needed to light a very dark surface brightly, while a pale surface requires less. If an actor is against a background that is a paler colour tone than his face, then he will need to be brighter than the background for the audience to focus on him with ease. A light face against a dark background is much easier to light and low lighting intensities can be used. By the same token, Caucasian skin is easier to light than Negro skin. It is particularly hard to light both equally when they appear together.

Because of the way the eye perceives light, a small sudden increase in light intensity will appear more powerful to the audience than a greater, slower increase; conversely, a slow decrease permits light to fall to very low levels while still allowing the audience to see. The lighting designer also needs to know that visual fatigue can set in if the light intensity is too bright or too dim for any length of time. Varying brightness can help overcome this and add dynamics to your lighting.

Diffusion

Natural lighting conditions rarely stay the same for long. There are constantly changing atmospheric conditions as well as changes in the relationship between the positions of the sun and the earth. A clear fine day one minute can be dull and cloudy the next. On a clear day, because there is no cloud cover to diffuse or soften the light from the sun, shadows appear strong and sharp. When there is cloud, shadows are softened to the point where they may be non-existent. Such a shadow-free world is lit with soft light or diffuse light. Often both types of light are present: strong sunlight may cast a crisp shadow of an object, but sunlight reflecting from other surfaces such as buildings diffuses and softens some of the crisp shadows.

Contrast

Contrast is another element the lighting designer needs to consider. When sunlight strikes a face from the front, both sides of the face will be evenly lit. If the light is coming from one side only, that side of the face will be more strongly lit than the other. Normally light striking other surfaces, such as a wall or the floor, will reflect light back onto the unlit side of the face, so that one side is lit by a single source while the other is lit by reflected or diffuse light. If there is no reflected light, the other side will remain in darkness.

The balance in intensity between the light and dark is known as contrast. On a cloudy day a face will be in low contrast (both sides will be evenly lit), whereas lit by a car headlamp at night, it will be in high contrast (one side bright, the other dark).

Texture

Light does not only reach us in unbroken beams. In a forest, sunlight shining through the branches will give a broken light that will dapple the forest floor. In a city, where walls and glass reflect light down onto street level, the light level will be uneven. It is quite normal for light to have such undulations of intensity; this is called its texture. When the texture is even (when there is little or no reflected or broken light) the light is said to be flat. Light such as this will be found in a large open space such as a field. Textured light is often achieved with the use of gobos (see page 72).

Colour

The use of colour is a very powerful tool for the lighting designer. We may think of light from the sun as being colourless, but it is coloured at all times of the day. Blue tones dominate at noon, pink and orange at sunset. In fact, sunlight is made up of a mixture of colours.

Light transmitted to earth is a small part of the total electromagnetic energy emitted by the sun. Visible electromagnetic energy (or the visible spectrum) is flanked on either side by ultra-violet light and infra-red light, both of which are invisible to the naked eye. Electromagnetic energy arrives at the earth in waves and each wavelength is measured by its frequency. The unit of measurement is the nanometre. Each individual frequency within the visible part of the spectrum defines a different colour. For instance blue has a wavelength of about 425N; green about 535N; and red about 650N. Combine all the visible

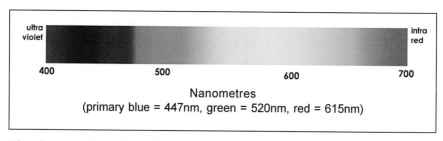

This diagram shows the visible part of the total electromagnetic spectrum. Each colour can be defined by its own wavelength.

frequencies together and you have white light. Separate them, and you have the individual colours of the spectrum.

To see this for yourself, you can do a simple experiment. Pass a beam of light through a prism and shine it onto a piece of white paper. The light emerging from the other side is refracted, or split, into the component parts of the spectrum – red, orange, yellow, blue, green, indigo and violet.

Just as we only see an object if light strikes it, so we only see the colour of an object if it is lit by light containing that object's colour. If not, it will not reflect the light and will appear to be black. So we can see any object by daylight because daylight contains all the colours of

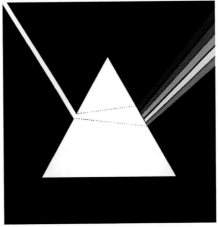

Pass a beam of white light through a glass prism and the beam will be divided into its component colours. The glass refracts each wavelength differently, which causes the colours to fan out. This shows that white light is a combination of all the colours in the spectrum.

the spectrum. On stage, a red object lit by green light will appear black. It must be lit by red (or white light) to be seen. Similarly a set, costume or make-up only looks alive if it is lit by lighting containing its colours. If not, it will appear dull and jaded or, in the extreme, unrealistic. So it is most common to light plays with the palest of tints as these contain all the colours of the spectrum and will light all coloured objects well, in addition to being close to the colour of natural light. Of course, there may be cases where you are looking for an unrealistic effect, and then strong-coloured lights may be just what are wanted. The lighting designer should also know that by lighting settings with similar tones of light to the colour of the paint finishes used, a sense of vibrancy can be created in the design.

The tricks light plays

There are many tricks that our eyes play on us. You need to be aware of them for sometimes they can be usefully harnessed on stage; similarly it is useful to know how light can be used to compensate for the inadequacies of our eyes.

For instance, at low intensity levels such as at night-time, it is easier to see blue light than any other colour. Reduce the light levels even lower and all colour recedes to grey. This greying of colour also occurs over a distance. Objects on the horizon will appear grey if the atmosphere is anything other than crystal clear.

Distance also affects three-dimensional form. An object will appear most three-dimensional the nearer it is to the viewer; as objects move away they become more two-dimensional.

Another trick of the eyes is that if you stare at a colour for a period of time, you start to think that the colour is becoming whiter or, in other words, becoming desaturated. If another colour is then introduced, the eye may become confused and not recognize the true value of the new colour. You can try this for yourself. For example, stare at a spot of red light for a minute. Now look at a spot of yellow light and the eye will think that the new colour is green. Only slowly will the eye adjust to the colour yellow.

So if a lighting designer uses a colour without change over a period of time, it will then take just the subtlest of shifts in the lighting to change that tone radically or to reinforce the existing tone.

Thus it is very important for the lighting designer to understand the properties of light and how the eye works and perceives lighting conditions. Any light source has qualities relating to its position, intensity, diffusion, contrast, texture and colour, and each of these needs to be considered and assessed in turn when deciding the correctness of any lantern within a stage composition.

3 CONTROLLING THE VARIABLES

In order to create a lighting design, you must have a full understanding of how to control and combine several variables: the position of the light source; the intensity of the light; and the texture and colour of the light. In controlling and combining these to create lighting compositions, called 'states', the lighting designer must also address how the states join together or flow into one another. These links or moments of change in the lighting are called 'cues'.

Position of the light source

The position of the light source or sources is probably the most important element to understand. Terms such as low side, side, high side, three-quarter backlight and toplight are often used to describe lighting positions, but they are rather imprecise. For greater accuracy you actually have to measure the angle from the object being viewed to the light source. This must be done because when you come to draw the lights of your choice on a lighting plan, you are categorically defining their relationship to the area they serve.

Thus, if a single light source is placed on the rig and shone on stage, its position can be defined as having a particular vertical angle to the stage floor and a particular horizontal angle to the centre line of the stage. These are its coordinates. They are important because they are used by the lighting designer when analyzing an idea or when specifying lighting positions to others in the production team.

The most important part of an actor to light will normally be the face. Depending on the position of the light source, the effect will vary, as the examples overleaf show.

If you want to achieve such effects, you must know the angles involved. This gives you the light's coordinates and will show you where to place your light source on the rig. In many cases there will be more than one source lighting an actor, so it becomes even more important to know the coordinates for each.

Once you know the angle you want, you have to know where to place a light on the rig to achieve this angle. For instance, if you wish to light an actor with a vertical light of, say, 45°, first draw a simple scale section of the theatre with the actor standing at the centre of the stage.

The effect of light on the face from differing angles

Straight on/V45° from the front

H45°/V45° from the front

Side/V45°

V45°/H45° from behind

(H = horizontal and V = vertical [beam angles])

Straight on/V45° from behind – backlight

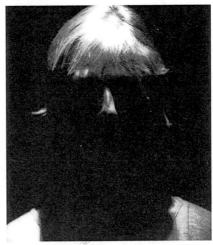

Directly above – toplight

Side/head height

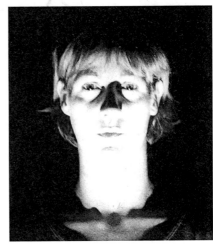

From below – footlight

Finding the position of a light source

Two angles define the position of a lantern hanging on a rig: an angle in the horizontal plane to a line running through the actor being lit parallel to the centre line of the stage; and an angle in the vertical plane to a line parallel to the stage floor running through the actor's eye line.

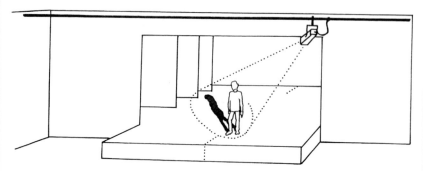

This can also be drawn as: and overhead view – a plan; and a side view – a section. These show the exact angle at which light strikes the actor in both planes.

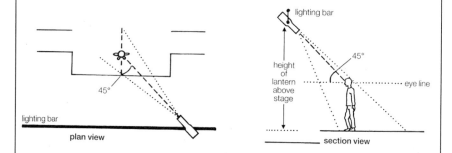

When combined on a lighting plan, the horizontal angle is defined by the position of the lantern on the bar (in relation to its centre of focus) and the vertical angle by the height of the bar (above the actor's eye line) and its distance from the focused position. In this example the lantern is at 45° / 45° to the actor.

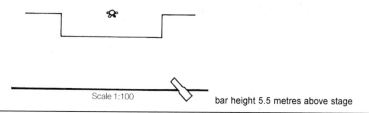

Draw a line parallel to the stage floor through the actor's eye level, then draw a second line from the eyes, 45° up from this. A lantern placed anywhere along the second line will give a 45° light. Position a lighting bar on the plan to intercept this line and draw the lantern on this bar.

You must allow for the fact that the lantern hangs about 25 centimetres (10 inches) below the bar. This light will now give an average value of 45° across the acting area. If the actor walks nearer the light, the angle gets a little steeper; as he walks away the angle gets a little shallower.

If you wish to position a lantern according to its horizontal angle, use the same technique.

Once you have found the position for a lantern you must choose one with a beam angle (spread of light) sufficiently great to cover the actor cube, that is to say, the three-dimensional space the actor occupies on stage. Measure the diagonal of the 'actor cube'. This is the measurement that the beam angle must cover. Normally the measurements given to an actor cube are 2.5 metres (8 feet) wide, by 2.5 metres (8 feet) deep, by 2 metres (6½ feet) high. In the case of an actor cube with these measurements, the diagonal measures approximately 4 metres (13 feet).

By drawing this diagonal into your section drawing, and drawing the edges of the beam to include the whole of this line, you will get an idea of the beam angle required to light this actor cube space. This method allows you to calculate the beam angle of every lantern on the rig. Once the rigging position and the area of stage to be lit are decided, draw a section in this manner to find the beam angle required.

If you are specifying a profile lantern (see p. 53), it is crucial to state what beam-angle lantern is needed as variable-beam profiles have limited beam-angle ranges. Pebble-convex lanterns or Fresnels (see pp. 55, 56) have such a wide beam-angle range that most eventualities are covered. Only when the throw, or distance of the lantern to the subject, is very short is it worth checking that these lanterns can deliver the required beam angle.

Ideally, a lighting designer wants to be able to position a lantern anywhere. Sometimes, though, a theatre's architecture prevents this. In the case of a proscenium-arch stage, the best positions for fixing lighting are overhead and to the sides of the stage, and overhead and to the sides of the auditorium. Sometimes though scenery or masking (the black flats or cloths used to hide backstage areas) may prevent these positions from being used. Theatres in the round often offer the widest range of possibilities, especially for overhead

Finding the beam angle for the 'actor cube'

A lantern lighting an actor normally is set at a beam angle to light an area a little larger than his body size. This can be thought of as a cube approximately 2.5m (8 ft) wide; 2.5m (8 ft) deep; and 2m (6½ ft) high, centred on the actor's stage position.

This beam angle is wide enough to allow the actor to move a little within the beam, but not too wide to preclude selective lighting of the stage.

For a lantern to light the whole 'actor cube', it must be set at a beam angle to light the length of the diagonal of the cube.

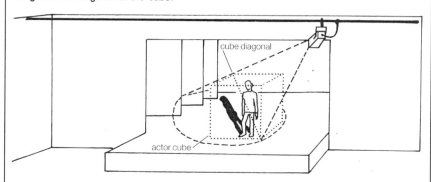

To work out the beam angle required to light the cube, draw a section of the situation (to scale). This must show: the height of the lantern above the stage; the distance of the lantern from the actor; and the length of the cube's diagonal, substituted for the actor.

Draw lines from the lantern to the ends of the diagonal (to represent the edges of the beam). Measure the angle between these lines to find the approximate beam angle required to light the cube.

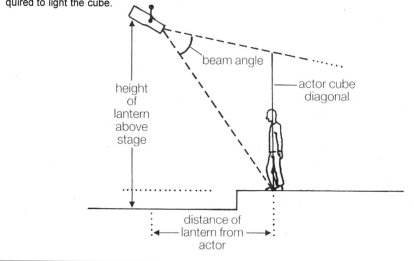

lighting. Here there is often less suspended or tall scenery to obstruct the beams of light, and the lighting bars can be quite closely spaced.

Intensity of light

Intensity of light is another factor for the lighting designer to consider. Obviously the brightness of a lantern's output is important here. The most common theatre lamps have wattages of 500 Watts, 575W, 650W, 1 kiloWatt, 1.2kW and 2kW. More specialist lamps have wattages above these. Providing lamps being compared are all members of the same family, say the tungsten-halogen family (see p. 61), then, for example a 2kW lamp is about four times as bright as a 500 watt lamp, and twice as bright as a 1kW lamp, although this also depends on the efficiency of the optics in the lantern.

You must also remember though that light from a single source diminishes in intensity the farther away it gets from its source. This is shown in the inverse square law. Double the distance a subject is from the light source and the brightness will quarter. It is normal for a manufacturer's catalogue to quote the intensity of light output of a lantern at 1 metre (3 feet). So, if a lantern has an intensity of 16,000 Lux at 1 metre (3 feet), at 2 metres (6½ feet) its intensity will be 4,000 lux, at 3 metres (9 feet) it will be 1,778 lux, and so on. Thus a profile lantern with a 22° beam angle and an intensity of 40,000 lux at 1 metre (3 feet), its intensity will be 2,500 lux at 4 metres (13 feet). Another with a 40° beam angle and intensity of 24,000 lux at 1 metre (3 feet) will have an intensity of 1,475 lux at 4 metres (13 feet)

What this means in practice is that the actor will always be brighter the nearer he is to the light source. But have him too close and this can give an unpleasant, over-bright, burnt-out effect.

There is one major inconvenience caused on stage by the fact that the intensity of a light diminishes as a beam spreads. The centre line of a proscenium-arch stage – the line that is the most powerful dramatically – is, on average, the farthest point from the lighting positions. Therefore the lighting of this line will need special care and treatment if it is to be lit at the same or greater intensity than the rest of the stage.

Another factor to consider is that if you colour a beam by using a gel (see Chapter 5), then the gel absorbs some of the light's intensity. The darker the colour of the gel, the more intensity is absorbed. For example, to project a deep blue brightly on stage will require a far more powerful lamp than for a pale-rose colour. The transmission of a gel (the percentage of light it transmits)

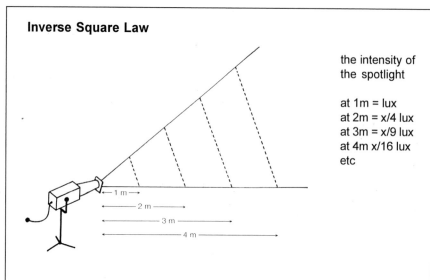

Inverse Square Law

the intensity of the spotlight

at 1m = lux
at 2m = x/4 lux
at 3m = x/9 lux
at 4m x/16 lux
etc

1 m
2 m
3 m
4 m

This law illustrates the principle of how intensity decreases as distance increases from a light source. Note also that the width of the beam doubles as distance from the light source doubles.

is stated in the manufacturer's swatch book (see p. 68) and is a useful guideline as to how much you need to increase your lantern power in order to project that colour as intensely as a paler colour or 'open white' (the term used to indicate no gel).

A further complication arises concerning the focus of a lantern. When in spot focus (narrow beam angle), the intensity of the light is much greater than when the same lantern is in flood focus (wide beam angle).

So the specification of a lantern to achieve a certain intensity is possibly the hardest calculation a lighting designer has to make as there are so many variables at play. It is impossible to give guidelines on what wattage to choose as every situation is different. The points to remember are: how bright is the scene in your imagination? What is the distance from the lantern to the stage? How wide is the beam angle? What is the transmission of the gel?

It is better to overestimate the intensity of light needed than to underestimate it. After all, a lantern can always be faded down on the dimmer, but remember that over dimming can cause colour shifts due to changes in colour temperature (see p. 60), and this may play havoc with the finished look.

Texture

As we saw in Chapter 2, in real life we rarely have light of even intensity. Instead we usually see things lit not only by direct light, but also by light reflected off neighbouring surfaces. The result is uneven or textured light, softer light with less contrast and fewer shadows.

Chapter 5 will show how instruments like gobos can be used to break up or change the texture of light. The structure and geometry of a set may provide lighting positions that will have a similar effect. For instance, light beams can break over items on stage or shine through open areas of a set such as windows and arches. Do not forget the use of backlighting through shutters and doorways too. This can look very dynamic.

The texture of the light may also be controlled by changes in the beam edge. A profile will give a tightly defined spot of light that only goes beyond its local area by reflection. Fresnels will light a designated area but will also send out scattered light to other stage areas. A stage lit exclusively with a hard-edge spotlight makes the actors look much crisper and sharper than if they were lit in soft-edge spots.

Shadowless lighting is very hard to achieve on stage because all conventional theatre lanterns cast hard shadows. Softlights (large-surface reflector lights) are manufactured for photographic, film and television purposes, but it is difficult to utilize them on stage because their light beams are too unfocussed. Although often impractical, soft light can sometimes be created by bouncing light off a white reflector in the wings, off a flat, or off a ceiling piece or the stage floor. Usually the best means of obtaining an excellent soft light on stage is with strip lighting in the footlight position or from immediately behind the top of the proscenium arch.

Colour

Colour is another variable that the lighting designer can control to achieve different effects. We have already seen how different colours can produce different emotional responses, and how white light is in fact made up of all the colours of the spectrum.

The lighting designer uses gels or filters (see Chapter 5) to colour beams of light. A gel works by allowing through only light from the colour spectrum that is common to the colour of the gel. A primary green gel lets through only green light; a yellow will let through red and green but none of the blue tones; a pale salmon lets through mostly red, but also a high percentage of green and blue.

On stage, when light beams coloured with different gels blend together, the resulting colour will be closer to white than the original gels. A true white can only be obtained if the colours of the spectrum are in equal proportion in the mixture, otherwise the result will be white with a hint of colour. True white is a highly prized commodity for the lighting designer because of its closeness to daylight and its emotional neutrality and ambiguity.

One way to achieve white light is by shining the three primaries – red, green and blue, from different lanterns onto a common surface. In fact, any colour can be obtained from the primaries simply by varying the intensities of these three colours. If you combine any two of the primaries, you make a secondary colour. Red and green make yellow, red and blue make magenta, and blue and green make a turquoise known as cyan. Again, if you mix all three secondaries together equally you will get white light. Similarly, if you mix a primary and the secondary of the other two primaries together you get white. These two colours are then called complementary. For example, red mixed with cyan gives white.

Mixing colours for stage lighting like this using gelled lanterns is known as additive colour mixing. The difficulty when designing a lighting scene is in selecting colours that speak for themselves in a composition, but can also be mixed to create the desired colour effects.

Two half-size gels can be placed side by side and sellotaped together to make a full gel. This version of additive mixing is very useful for mixing new, original colours. This works best in profile lanterns: in a pebble-convex lantern or fresnel, the original colours are seen side by side.

If more than one coloured gel is overlaid in the same lantern, then the beam colour moves towards black. This is called subtractive colour mixing and is a less useful way of mixing colour because it reduces the output of light. This technique is only useful for mixing the very palest of tints. Here little light will be lost because of the very high transmissions of the gels used.

If you are running a lantern dimmed to a low-intensity level, it will have a very yellow light because its colour temperature has been lowered. If this beam is then coloured, the 'yellow' lamp will subtractively mix with the gel. It is vital to know this because if a blue gel is used, the colours will cancel each other out (because blue and yellow are complementaries) and the result will be a dirty grey beam. This dirty grey light can be a useful part of the designer's palette, but if you wish to maintain the strength of the original colour, lanterns must be run at as high a dimmer level as possible.

How coloured light works on stage

This diagram shows that when red, green and blue lights (the primary colours) are shone from three different sources, where two overlap a new colour is created (called the secondary), and that whit light is made where all three overlap. Making new colours in this manner is called additive colour mixing.

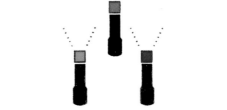

Shine a beam of white (or full spectrum) light onto a surface and only light of the same colour as the surface will be reflected (thus allowing us to see its colour). It will appear black if the beam does not contain the same colour (for example a green surface will appear black under red or blue light). Therefore, a set or costume will appear dull or jaded unless lit with light that includes similar colours.

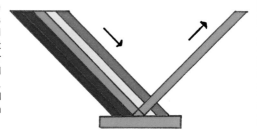

Mixing colours on the face

L = Lee Filters, # = Rosco Supergel

L154 ↗   ↖ #04

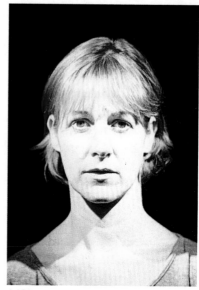

L103 ↗   ↖ L117

#74 ↗   ↖ L203

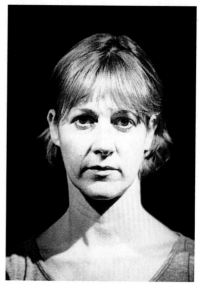

L202 ↗   ↖ L203

In each of these examples, two lanterns of equal intensity are used, positioned at 45° horizontal / 45° vertical on either side of the face.

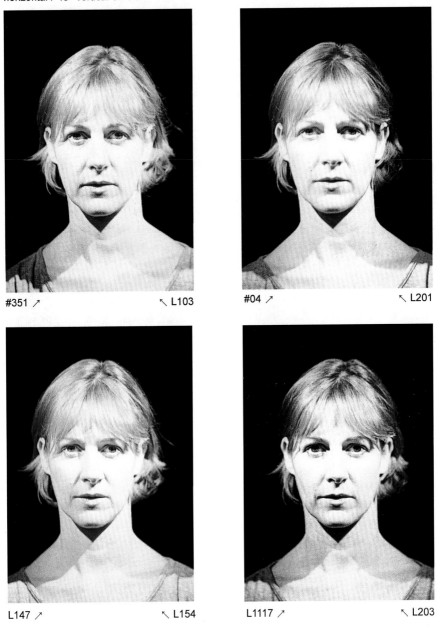

#351 ↗   ↖ L103   #04 ↗   ↖ L201

L147 ↗   ↖ L154   L1117 ↗   ↖ L203

Subtle effects with pale colours

It is also interesting to note how warm and cool tones mix when used together. If you shine straw (warm) and steel blue (cool) from different lanterns onto the actor, where they meet they produce white. This is because the straw colour is a paler version of yellow, while the steel blue is a paler version of blue, and blue and yellow are complementaries.

This is very useful indeed, especially when setting up lights 45° front and from either side (see Chapter 7) – accepted as good positions for a naturalistic style of lighting. Colour one side warm and the other cool. When used together they will give white faces with one warm side and the other cool.

The result of this can be very enigmatic – half happy, half sad. With subtle control of the dimmers, one look can be made to dominate. Lighting like this is commonly used, especially in 'classic' texts, as it offers a wide range of emotional interpretations to support and develop the work of the actor.

Open white light, that is light without any coloured filter or gel is a neutral colour, and is useful either to lighten other colour tones or as the starting point when working out the dominant colour for a production.

Lavenders are also useful and feel neutral. Lavender is a mix of pale pink and blue and gives a very pleasing soft white. This can be substituted for open white to give a more delicate and intimate tone. It will appear warm when set against cool colours and cool when contrasted with warms. (See pages 34-35).

Composition

All of these elements come together when the lighting designer creates lighting compositions or 'states'. Of course a state will reflect the mood of the moment, the actors' positions on stage and the set itself. But there are also principles to apply for the creation of good compositions.

A trip to an art gallery can be a useful starting point. Artists through the centuries have used light as a means of helping the viewer understand and appreciate the painting. Light can be used to show depth in a picture; order and hierarchy in the groupings of subjects; the focus of attention; and it can be used equally well to show areas of importance.

These tried and tested principles should be absorbed by the theatre lighting designer and harnessed in the context of the play in question (see following pages).

Describing light with the aid of pictures

Saint Francis in Meditation (Francisco de Zurbaran).
Reproduced courtesy of the Trustees, the National Gallery, London.

To achieve a similar effect to this on stage, a single bright lantern would be placed in the stage right wing with a vertical angle of about 45° and focused to a tight soft-edged pool around the actor and coloured with a very pale straw gel. There is also a little reflected light inside the hood to dimly light the saint's face. This simple use of light creates a most powerful image.

An equally important use of light for this painting lies in the treatment of the background: the wall is unlit on the saint's bright side, yet it is softly lit behind his unlit side, casting his body into silhouette. This simple technique greatly increases the three-dimensional aspect as well as adding visual interest.

Describing light with the aid of pictures

Marriage à la Mode: The Killing of the Earl (William Hogarth).
Reproduced courtesy of the Trustees, the National Gallery, London.

This very theatrical painting employs light to draw attention to the most important aspects of the composition.

There are three light sources in the picture: the main source which appears to come from a fireplace; a candle near the window; and a hand-held lantern. Each light source casts a very specifically focused light illuminating a particular grouping of figures. The three distinct areas suggest there is little else of importance in the room.

The light is neither coloured nor textured (although the lantern casts a shadow of its holder on the ceiling). It is a simple control of focus that aids the storytelling of this picture.

Describing light with the aid of pictures

The Finding of Moses (Nicholas Poussin).
Reproduced courtesy of the Trustees, the National Gallery, London.

This picture illustrates how light can be used to create the impression of depth in a composition. The main subjects are localised and sculpted in the foreground by a bright, sharp beam (coming from the left) that creates quite a high contrast on the faces as there is little reflected light. The trees and rocks of the midground lie in silhouette. The background is well lit, but less brightly than the foreground. So, intensity and hardness/softness of light is graded from foreground to background. Note also that the background colours recede to grey – which also aids the impression of distance.

Describing light with the aid of pictures

Bathers (Paul Cézanne).
Reproduced courtesy of the Trustees, the National Gallery, London.

This bathing scene illustrates many varied aspects of light. There is strong use of warm amber and blue tones throughout the picture. Sources from either side of the painting light each bather in these colours. This flattering colouration helps show their soft, rounded forms. Those in the foreground are predominantly amber, whereas those further back are increasingly blue. Colour finally recedes to blue-grey for the horizon of surrounding trees.

Across the whole picture, light is broken. This creates a dappled feel as if it is filtering through foliage. However, its intensity is even – or flat – across the whole painting, with no subjects highlighted. This gives an open, spacious feel despite the proximity of the trees.

Dealing with cues

Next you have to decide how to change from one state to another, in other words how to create the cues. Whether the cues are required by a scene change, to indicate the passage of time, or to allow changes of light to highlight certain aspects of the text, you must be clear how you want them to look. You may choose to have your cues as punctuation points – for example using a blackout between scenes, or you may want to be more fluid – simply by fading from one state to the next, which is called 'cross fading'.

If you choose a fluid fade, the rate of fade will have a fade time, and if you choose to go via blackout, there may be a wait time before the next state fades in. A cue where change is completed instantly is called a 'snap'. Cues are timed in seconds (or minutes and seconds). The new incoming lighting state has an 'up' time and the existing state going out has a 'down' time.

If a crossfade is completed seamlessly, it is called a 'dipless crossfade'. If the crossfade dims in the middle, a useful method of punctuating a change in time without going to the extreme of blackout, it is called a 'dipped crossfade'.

When one cue triggers another, they are said to 'link' or 'follow on'. Occasionally, perhaps to highlight the main character, lights will come up on a single actor before the whole picture appears. Here the second lighting picture follows on from the first and there may be a build of levels, in other words an increase of the initial state rather than a crossfade. The reverse may happen at the end of a scene. The stage picture checks down to a single spot on the main actor before following on to a blackout.

Occasionally, several cues will happen at the same cue point, with lights coming on each with different fade times. This is called a 'move fade'. Changes of pace within the fade, for example a fade starts slowly but speeds up as the light diminishes, give the fade what is called a 'profile'.

Cues can be so subtle that the audience does not realize they are happening. In the course of a scene, for example, lighting may become localized around the lead actors for emphasis, or highlights may subtly change as the emphasis shifts from actor to actor. The sun may set during the course of an act. Here one lighting state (mid-afternoon) is plotted (see Chapter 4) for the opening of the act and a second state, with the sun now low in the sky, is plotted for the end. A fade time equal to the length of the act is allocated to the cue, and the cue is triggered as soon as the lights fade up at the start of the act. The change will then occur during the act and the new state will be reached as the act finishes. Other cues can still be run during the act over the top of this cue, for example changes to emphasize certain actors, to reflect their moves around a set or to suggest emotional changes.

The mode chosen for the cues can have a profound influence on the style of the production. Snapping lights on at the start of a scene indicates a different performance style from that of a slow, gentle fade-up. The designer must have a full understanding of the conventions and how they vary between different performance genres.

4 THE EQUIPMENT

Compared to other applications of artificial light, for instance domestic and industrial, today's theatre has to harness and control light in a very sophisticated way. Indeed, so sophisticated has stage lighting become that recent trends in architectural, display and leisure lighting have borrowed techniques from theatre lighting. The main components of the theatre lighting system are the power supply, the control desk, the dimmer system, the lanterns and the light source. Whether the theatre has a large or small lighting facility, all five components will be present – only the amount of equipment varies.

The power supply

One of the greatest constraints facing the lighting designer is the amount of power that is available in a venue, because this will restrict the size of a rig and the brightest lighting state. To calculate the available power, the designer must understand the three units of measurement of electricity: volts, amps and watts. Voltage refers to the mode in which power travels to an appliance; amperage refers to the amount of power that is available; and wattage refers to the amount of power an appliance uses. The three units are related to each other by the following formula show in box below.

$$volts = \frac{watts}{amps}$$

This can also be expressed as:

$$watts = volts \times amps$$

or:

$$amps = \frac{watts}{volts}$$

Application of this formula is necessary for all the basic calculations concerning safe loading of a system.

When applying the formula in the UK, the figure of 240 is substituted for volts as the UK supply is 240 volts. To use this formula in any country other than the UK, simply substitute the local mains voltage for 240 volts.

In UK homes the square-pinned 13 amp socket is the norm, meaning that 13 amps is the amount of power that is available to be used from that socket.

If you were lighting a play in a small

venue such as a school hail, there might only be a single 13 amp socket available to power the rig, so you would need to work out how many lighting appliances can be run from a 13 amp socket. A 500 watt lantern uses 500 watts of power, so using the formula, the total amount of watts used can be found:

$$W = V \times A \qquad W = 240 \times 13 \qquad W = 3120$$

Therefore up to 3,120 watts of power can be drawn from a 13 amp socket. And in the case of the 500 watt lantern, this means six can be run at the same time and at full intensity from one 13 amp point (6 x 500 = 3,000). There is 120 watts spare capacity, so try to run seven lanterns and the system will be overloaded (7 x 500 = 3,500). The result will be a blown fuse, or a tripped circuit breaker.

The 13 amp plug contains a fuse, and a fuse of the next higher amperage rating than the appliance being used should be fitted, up to a maximum of 13 amps. The 15 or 16 amp round-pin plug used in the UK theatre has no fuse: instead the fuse, or on more modern equipment a circuit-breaker, is located at the dimmer. This is because often several plug and sockets occur in hooking a lantern up to a dimmer, and fuse changing would be very time consuming.

Moreover, the standard cable that is used in theatre lighting is rated at 10 amp capacity. This means that up to 2.4kW of lanterns can be run through it, but not more. Therefore, even though a plug may be rated at 15 amps, it should not be loaded above the 10 amp capacity of the cable. Devices to pair lanterns together on one cable are called 'grelcoes' (the multi-socket adaptor) or 'splitters' (simply two cables joined in a plug). Whenever pairing lanterns together, no more than 2.4kW of lantern power should accumulate onto a single 10 amp cable.

Further investigation is still needed though to find the capacity of a lighting system. If a theatre has 60 x 10 amp dimmers, it does not necessarily mean that this capacity can be fully loaded (600 amps – a very large power supply – would be needed to power them to full capacity). The amount of power going into each dimmer rack needs to be found. This is usually marked on the labelling on the switch gear for the dimmer packs. In a small installation perhaps only 32 amps will feed each pack of six dimmers. This would mean that only 7.6kW of lanterns could be run (at the same time and at full intensity) from each pack – although 2.4kW could still be run from any single 10 amp dimmer. A larger installation may have 63 amps per six ways of dimming – this will allow full loading of the dimmer rack to 10 amps per dimmer. On permanent installations where dimmer packs containing twenty dimmers are found, it is common for each pack to be fed by 63 amps – or an average loading of 750 watts per dimmer; or if fed by 100 amps, then an average loading of 1,200 watts per dimmer. Of course it is unusual to have all dimmers fully loaded and running at full at the same time on a theatre show, but total loadings on racks at all times must be considered or else the dimmers will fuse or 'trip' out.

A final word on installations concerns electrical phasing and their safe usage. Electricity is normally distributed as three separate supplies or phases. The three phases are separated at the incoming mains distribution board. It is standard practice to treat each phase as a separate supply that must not come into contact with either of the other two phases through cable, metalwork or any other conductors of electricity. This means that power from one phase must not go to sockets that are connected to another phase, nor should any temporary cabling join the phases. This is because when phases are joined, a higher voltage can be present than is possible from a single phase and a shock from this voltage normally proves lethal. Thus, in a theatre with a proscenium-arch stage, one phase might go to the front-of-house lighting, one to overhead on stage, and the third to stage floor and wings. No circuits from one phase should be redistributed to increase circuits in another part of the theatre, in other words there should be no 'crossing the phases'. A theatre's lighting plan should show clearly how the phasing is distributed, and sockets should be colour-coded red, yellow and blue to indicate which phase the socket is connected to.

Studio theatres where staging varies can be more complicated in the way phases are distributed and extra care should be taken here. Such complications do not occur in single-phase venues, although these are usually only the smallest. Wherever the designer is working, the implications of phase distribution must be considered as well as the amount of power that is available. There is no point coming up with a wonderful design if there is not enough power to feed it or if it creates dangerous conditions on stage.

Whatever you do, make sure that electrical work is only carried out by those qualified to do so. Always have your designs checked for safety by a qualified person before it is rigged. All theatres should have maintenance and safety testing programmes in place for regular checking of equipment. For your own information, keep abreast of changes to the regulations in electrical practice by referring to the latest edition of the IEE wiring regulations book or contacting specialist organisations such as ABTT for advice (see Further Reading).

Otherwise, contact a specialist in theatre lighting, such as the resident chief electrician.

The control desk

Lighting control is provided by a unit known as the control desk. This can be either manually or computer operated, and some desks have both options. Although computer-memory control, introduced in the 1970s, is now the norm in professional theatres, many installations, in particular schools or smaller venues, still use manual control. The great advantage of the manual desk is its speed of use, especially when small-scale improvisation is called for. The advantage of computer control is the accurate recording and playback of complex cue sequences.

A manual control desk has a master fader controlling the overall level of the control desk and one fader per dimmer. This allows for individual level setting of each dimmer, but there is also the possibility of coordinated raising and lowering of the whole lighting state. Faders are arranged in several ranks, called presets, that allow the next lighting states to be set up in advance. When it is time for the cue, just the master faders need to be moved to generate the new lighting picture. However, setting up the presets takes one's attention from the play and the time this takes reduces the possibility of running many cues in a short space of time. A manual control desk may also have some features such as grouping switches to preset within a preset, switches for instant blackout, and timed faders for automatic control of crossfades.

With a computer-memory control desk, a lantern's dimmer number is typed in and the intensity level for the dimmer is specified as a percentage. When the whole lighting state has been set up in this manner, it is given a memory number and fade time and all is stored in the desk's memory by pressing a 'record' button. At the touch of a 'go' button, the lighting state can be recalled and automatically faded in. This means that the designer has much more scope for rapid recall of states, as well as the possibility for great variations in fade time. This type of desk also allows greater precision: there are up to 100 subdivisions of a lantern's intensity level — accuracy that a manual desk cannot match. In addition, long fades can be smoothly executed, something even the best manual-desk operator cannot guarantee.

Computer-memory control desks also have many other useful features. These include move fades – the ability to run more than one cue at a time and with different fade times; sophisticated chase sequences for pulsing lights in various

Diagram of a 12-way 2-preset manual control desk
LX manual lighting control desk Strand Lighting

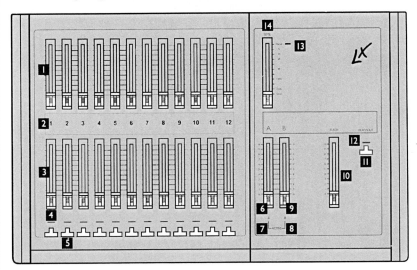

A guide to the control desk

1 'A' preset faders	4 channel indicator LEDs	7 'A' preset active LED	10 flash level fader	13 manual crossfade
2 'write-on' label	5 channel flash buttons	8 'B' preset active LED	11 blackout switch	indicator LED
3 'B' preset faders	6 'A' master fader	9 'B' master fader	12 blackout LED	14 crossfade time fader

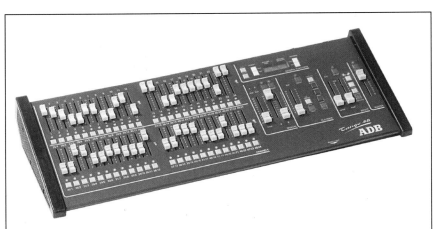

Tango 48 lighting control desk
ADB-TTV Technologies

LX
Strand Lighting

300 Series
Strand Lighting

Spark 4d
Compulite GB / Stagetech

Express
ETC Europe

Frog
Zero 88

Level Plus manual desk
Zero 88

patterns; soft-patching channels on the desk to dimmers, for logical organisation (similar to manual patching, see p. 65, but an electronic version); and the control of devices such as colour scrollers (see p. 71). In addition, computer-memory control desks can store the lighting for an entire show on the hard disc or on a floppy, disks can be modified on a PC and a printer can be attached to allow for printouts of states and cues to be made.

Many desks today combine the best of both systems – manual faders for plotting combined with the keyboard and microprocessor for memory storage of states. A combination control desk is very common in small venues and in theatres in educational establishments where many types of performance are required and where operators of varying degrees of skill are found.

The dimmer system

The dimmer unit links the control desk to the lanterns and allows the setting of intensity levels for individual lights. Dimmers are usually located away from the stage as they need good ventilation and can be quite noisy.

Portable dimmers normally have six individual dimmer units in a case or rack. Each dimmer has a single or double plug to allow lanterns to be connected and is fitted with a 10 amp fuse or a circuit breaker. In the UK, up to 2.4kW of lights can be run off each dimmer, if the power supply allows this.

Permanent installations may have twenty dimmers in each rack and again, modern units have a circuit breaker fitted to each dimmer rather than a fuse.

The mode of control from the control desk to the dimmer rack can be either analogue or digital. An analogue control supply sends a variable low-voltage (normally 0-10 volts) to each dimmer via its own dedicated cable. Although this is a relatively cheap method of linking the control desk to the dimmers, in large systems it will involve bulky cable runs that hinder the portability of the control desk.

Different manufacturers use different voltages to power analogue dimmers from the control desk. When connecting systems together, always check for compatibility first. Most use a 0 to +10 volt system; however, some use a 0 to -10 volt system.

In a digital system, the desk sends a digital signal in binary code to the dimmers. A single two-core-plus earth cable carries all these signals where they are decoded to control dimmer level. This system allows for much quicker fitting up of equipment than an analogue link and easy repositioning if necessary of the control desk. If the lighting control desk gives out a digital signal, but the

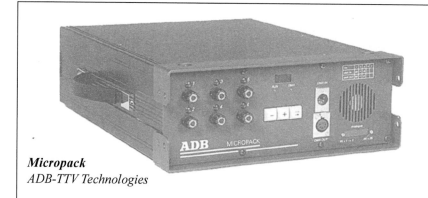

Micropack
ADB-TTV Technologies

Betapack
Zero 88

Smart Pack
ETC Europe

Demux
Zero 88

Reflection DMX backup
ETC Europe

Linebacker
Zero 88

dimmers work from analogue signals, then a demultiplex unit (known as a 'demux') must be fitted at the dimmer racks to configure the digital signal to an analogue one.

Digital dimmers have some advantages over analogue dimmers, with more stable and consistent fades. Advanced models can also 'talk' to the control desk to monitor their performance and report on faults. They can be set to control lamps other than 240 volts, for example 12 volt lamps, and can dim lamps such as fluorescent lamps, which cannot be dimmed by an analogue dimmer without extra control gear.

The protocol, or language, for sending the digital signal from the control desk to the digital dimmers has now been fully standardised. The protocol is called DMX 512, which means a maximum of 512 control channels can be operated for a single system. DMX 512 can also be used to control other items of equipment, such as moving lights, smoke machines and colour scrollers, which allows the control desk to operate a wide range of equipment.

MIDI (Musical Instrument Digital Interface) is another new type of control protocol, and many control desks are now fitted with a five-pin DIN plug for MIDI connection. MIDI is the most useful control protocol to use when the control desk has to be triggered either by an external source – for example a musician's keyboard – or when the control desk itself has to trigger external equipment such as sound sources. This makes MIDI well suited to multimedia and exhibition work.

The lanterns

The lantern, also sometimes called luminaire, is the housing that contains the lamp. In addition, it contains an optical system for controlling the delivery of the light to the stage. There are five different optical systems: profile, pebble-convex, fresnel, parcan and beamlight, and flood, each giving a different quality of light according to factors such as the diameter of the beam, the intensity of the beam, the texture of the edge of the beam and the evenness of light across the beam.

Within each family there is a choice of beam angle and of powers – normally a larger lantern indicates a more powerful instrument. All lanterns can be under-hung or over-rigged on a lighting bar using a hook clamp. They can also be rigged to a lighting stand with a spigot or to a vertical bar (or boom) with a boom arm. Once secured, a safety chain (or safety wire bond) should be attached for added security. If it is not obvious which way up a lantern should go, remember the colour frame will fall out if it is upside down. All lanterns have a lamp, reflector, cable with a plug connector, and most have one or two lenses, although this varies between optical systems. To add colour, a gel is fitted into a colour frame, and then slotted into the colour frame runners at the front of the lantern. The body of the lantern is connected to the hook clamp by a yoke. Horizontal movement of the lantern (or pan) is controlled by a nut or wing nut and bolt that join the yoke to the hook clamp. Vertical movement (or tilt) is controlled by the tilt lock that joins the yoke to the body. Both should be tightened or 'locked off' once the lantern has been set. When rigging a lantern leave enough slack cable to allow it to be panned and tilted when being focused.

Profiles

The characteristic output of a profile lantern is a hard-edged or defined, circular spot of light. To achieve this it uses one or two plano-convex lenses. With a single lens the beam will be at a fixed angle; with two independently moving lenses there can be a variable beam angle. Older single-lens lanterns allow for a second fixed lens to be fitted, which offers a second, wider beam angle. Focusing will set the size of the beam (for a two-lens lantern) and the sharpness of the edge of the beam.

Optique
Strand Lighting

SL 19
Strand Lighting

A59Z
ADB-TTV Technologies

Acclaim Zoomspot
Selecon

Freedom 28/58
CCT Lighting

Europe DS105
ADB-TTV Technologies

Most profiles also have a field adjuster underneath the lamp to allow the lamp to be set for either a bright-centre beam, called 'peaky' or an even-intensity beam called 'flat'. A slot found on top of the profile is called the gate. There are four shutters that are inserted at the gate to square off the edges of the beam. An iris can also be fitted into the gate to make the beam size smaller. A gobo and/or gobo rotator can be fitted into the gate (see Chapter 5) as well.

There are three variations on the standard profile:

(1) A variation on the two-lens profile has a third, fixed lens in front of the lamp. This is known as a 'condenser profile', and this lantern produces a much crisper beam which is particularly good for sharp gobo projection (see Chapter 5).

(2) In the last ten years a new type of profile has been launched called a 'Source Four Profile'. These lanterns have facilities in common with other profiles, but where they differ is that they have a highly efficient optical system in which the lamp is mounted in a horizontal plane (whereas most other lanterns have the lamp mounted vertically). As well as having a very clean, crisp beam, the extra optical efficiency of these lanterns mean that lower powered lamps can be used, saving energy and costs. Typically these lanterns use a 575W lamp, which is equivalent in brightness to a 1kW lamp in a conventional profile. These lanterns are made in both fixed beam and variable beam options.

(3) A follow spot is a type of profile lantern used for manually following the actor around the stage. It is fitted with an iris to regulate the beam size and a colour magazine for live colour changes.

Pebble-convex lanterns

1kW PC
Selecon

The pebble-convex lantern (PC) has a beam similar to a profile in soft-edge focus but is a lot cheaper than a profile. Its slightly pebbled lens gives the soft edge to the beam. It offers a beam-angle range from a tight narrow spot through to a flood. It has barndoors that can shape the beam, though not as precisely as the shutters on a profile.

Although pebble-convex lanterns perform well when focused in a tight narrow spot, they can be a little dead in the centre of the beam when used in flood mode. However, because they can be focused very quickly, have a useful soft-edged beam similar to a de-focused profile, and a wide range of beam angles, they can be a good alternative to a profile.

Fresnel lanterns

The Fresnel lantern (that takes its name from the Frenchman who originally developed the lens for use in lighthouses) is mainly used for creating pools of light for the acting area. Its lens is plano-convex: pebbled on the plano side and heavily cut into on the convex side to form a series of steps. A Fresnel can be focused to give anything from a tight spot of light to a wide flood. The edge of the beam is much softer than a pebble-convex lantern, its bright centre gently diminishing to nothing. Fresnels look very similar to PCs — only the distinctive lens distinguishes them.

Quartet Fresnel
Strand Lighting

Starlette 1kW Fresnel
CCT Lighting

As with the pebble-convex lantern a rotating barndoor attachment can be fitted to the front to shape the beam and control any unwanted spill of light.

Parcans and beamlights

These lanterns are the best choice when stabbing beams are required. The parcan was introduced in the 1970s and its impact on theatre lighting has been enormous. It consists of a sealed beam lamp containing a built-in lens and reflector similar to a car headlight, all housed in a simple container. There is no lens, so it cannot be focused. The lamp comes in a variety of beam-angle options, and the lamp unit is changed according to the desired beam width. The beam edge is soft and the centre very bright; the beam shape is oval rather than circular. The lamp can be rotated in the lantern to correctly orientate the oval beam shape.

PAR 64
James Thomas Engineering

Beamlite 500
Strand Lighting

Source 4 Multipar
ETC Europe

The reasons for the Parcan's popularity are many. It has an intense light beam that makes it particularly good for projecting deep colours; it is quick to rig and focus; it is very light in weight, so good for touring, and it is inexpensive. The parcan has become the standard unit for lighting pop groups and is also very common in the theatre, particularly for musicals and dance where intense light beams are often required. Barndoors can be fitted to control the spread of light.

Par lamps come in a variety of beam intensities and widths, each known by a number, such as Par 36. This refers to the diameter of the lens in eighths of an inch. The standard theatre unit is the 1kW Par 64 that comes in four beam-width options – the CP60 – 9° x 12°; the CP61 – 10° x 14°; the CP62 – 11° x 24°; the CP95 – 70° x 70°.

It is common to find American 120 volt parcans in the UK. These lamps are brighter than the UK 240 volt equivalent and offer a further range of beam angles. However, when used in the UK they must be rigged wired in pairs and connected in series (to equal 240 volts). Par 64 lamps in 120 volt versions come as No. 1s, which have a beam angle of 6° x 12°; No. 2s, which have a beam angle of 7° x 14°; No. 5s, 12° x 28°; and No. 6s, 24° x 48°.

A recent variation is the development of the Source Four Par. As with the Source Four profile, the lantern utilises a 575W horizontally mounted lamp, and is very bright while being a much smaller unit than

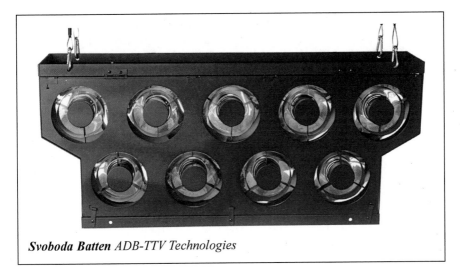

Svoboda Batten ADB-TTV Technologies

the 1kW parcan. Consequently, they are a very popular choice. To change beam angle, they are supplied with a range of clip-on plastic lenses that give a range of beam angles similar to a conventional parcan, from very narrow to very wide.

The beamlight gives a similar light quality to a parcan when in spot focus, but uses a conventional lamp with a double reflector system to gather the light. Although it has largely been superseded by the parcan, the beamlight has found a new lease of life as a soft-edged followspot currently in vogue with many lighting designers. The beamlight will also focus to a wide angle similar to a fresnel, but is most useful in spot focus when it is used for stabbing beams or for effects such as sunlight streaming through a window.

Up to ten beamlight-style lamps can be fitted side-by-side into a batten. Developed by the Czech designer, Josef Svoboda, these lanterns are called light curtains and give a dramatic high-powered sheet of light. They can also be fitted with motorized tilt and with colour changers. Another version, developed by Howard Eaton, fitted with 12-volt dichroic lamps is called a 'Howie batten'.

Floodlights

A floodlight is used when a beam of even intensity is required over a large area. It is simply a lamp with a reflector, and the reflector may be symmetrical or asymmetrical. The flood has no lens, but it can be coloured with a gel. It can only be panned or tilted and the beam angle cannot be controlled. Older

AC1001 Cyc Flood
ADB-TTV Technologies

floodlights such as the Strand 'Patt. 60', designed to accept tungsten lamps, are very bulky and inefficient. Modern floods designed around the linear 'K' class tungsten-halogen lamp are more efficient and compact.

The older Patt 60's as well as newer halogen floods have symmetrical reflectors. These are used when an even beam from all around the lantern is required – such as a toplight flood over a stage.

Asymmetrical reflector floods, such as the Coda or AC1001, are used to light cycloramas (the plain or painted cloth used at the back of a stage) because the asymmetrical shape of the reflectors is designed to reflect the light evenly down the cloth. A unit with a symmetrical reflector would make the area of the cloth nearest the lantern over bright.

Individual floods may be grouped together in a batten or, if at floor level, in a unit called a 'groundrow'. These grouped floods are used to give multicolour lighting of cycloramas.

The light source

At the heart of every lantern is its light source. The power of a lamp determines a lantern's brightness. But different types of lamp give off a different colour light according to their colour temperature. Like sunlight, light from a conventional theatre lamp is also a by-product of heat – electric power has heated the filament of the lamp so that it emits the visible light we harness, as well as a huge amount of heat or invisible infra-red light. This is called incandescence. An electric bar fire, as well as giving out heat in the form of invisible infra-red light also emits visible light – which will colour a room red at night. So the sun, a theatre lamp and an electric bar fire all produce light by a similar process, yet the colour of their light is different in each case. The electric fire gives off a red/orange glow; the theatre lamp emits a straw/yellow colour, while the light from the sun is a blue/white.

The reason for this light-colour emission is that they have all been heated to a different temperature. Thus the colour of a light source can be classified by its colour temperature, and this in turn acts as a reference to the whiteness of the light.

Chart to show different colour temperature values

7000 K	daylight	3200 k	CP class lamp at 100%intensity
6000 k	HMI/CID lamp	3000 k	TH class lamp at 100%
5000 k	carbon arc	2800 k	domestic lightbulb
4500 k	electronic photoflash	2750 k	TH class lamp at 65%
4500 k	metal halide lamp	2500 k	TH class lamp at 50%
4000 k	CSI lamp	2200 k	high pressure sodium lamp
3500 k	tungsten photoflood	2000 k	candle
3400 k	mercury blended lamp	1750 k	low pressure sodium lamp

all measures in degrees Kelvin

Note
a: a colour temperature difference of less than 200K cannot be noticed by the human eye.
b: Colour filters can be used to convert a light source from one colour temperature to another
(see page 70)

Colour temperature is defined thus: a black rod or poker, called a 'blackbody', is heated until it starts to glow or incandesce. The colour of the light at this point (red/orange) is noted, along with the temperature of the rod. More heat is applied and the colour moves through yellow to white, and then to blue. Whenever a colour change is detected, the new temperature and colour are noted. A measurement of around 5,000 Kelvin or K (the unit of measurement) is the closest to white or colourless light; below this and the light will be more yellow/red; above it and the light will be more blue.

The following table gives some idea of the different colour temperature values of some natural and artificial light sources.

It is crucial for a lighting designer to know the colour temperature of a light source because if different ones are combined on stage, various different shades of white will be seen and these are not always desirable. Similarly, the same colour filter placed in front of light sources of different colour temperatures will produce slightly different colours. Also, as a theatre lamp is dimmed, so its colour temperature falls. Thus, dimming a too powerful lantern to achieve the intensity of light required will give light of a different colour temperature to that of a lower-powered lantern running at full intensity. This means it is important to assess accurately the power of a lantern in the context of its use, as a low-powered lantern running at full power will give a beam of a different colour to a high-powered lantern dimmed down to the same intensity.

There are two main families of lamp found in theatre lanterns, incandescent (tungsten-halogen) and discharge lamps (fluorescent, metal halide, etc.). These two not only vary in how the light is produced, but also in how they are powered, in the intensity and quality of the light emitted, and in their colour temperature. All incandescent lamps will dim via conventional theatre dimmers; dimming discharge lamps is a more complex electronic or mechanical operation.

The incandescent or tungsten-halogen lamp

This is the most common theatre lamp. It consists of a quartz glass bulb containing a tungsten wire filament supported on two posts and set in a vacuum. When a voltage is applied to the lamp, the resistance of the filament causes it to heat up and give off light. The amount of light the lamp emits can be controlled by varying the voltage applied to it – as happens when the lamp is controlled by a theatre dimmer.

Various colour-temperature lamps are made for the tungsten halogen family – the most common theatre lamps being the T/H class (3,000K), and the CP class (3,200K).

The tungsten-halogen lamp has developed from the domestic tungsten lamp, which have rather too low a colour temperature for most theatre work. Also, the glass blackens as the lamp ages, lowering its light output. This occurs because the tungsten filament slowly evaporates and is deposited on the glass.

The tungsten-halogen lamp has a slightly higher colour temperature, and is a little 'whiter' in colour appearance. Also the glass does not blacken with age because a halogen such as iodine is added which stops the evaporated tungsten becoming deposited on the glass. In fact, the tungsten is deposited back onto itself, thus extending the life of the lamp. Their compact filament concentrates the light and so gives improved optical efficiency.

The disadvantages of the tungsten-halogen lamp are that they cannot achieve daylight colour temperatures, and that they are inefficient users of electricity – only about 10 per cent of the electricity is converted into light, the other 90 per cent is given out as heat.

The discharge lamp

This family, some of which are more common to the theatre than others, includes fluorescent lighting, metal halide, mercury, high-and low-pressure sodium, and lamps called HMI, CID and CSI. These lamps can be extremely powerful and some produce a higher colour temperature than filament lamps – much nearer to the white light desired by the theatre lighting designer. All convert electricity into light far more efficiently than incandescent lamps, and there can be considerable energy cost savings where these lamps are used.

However, none of the discharge lamps can be dimmed directly by a conventional theatre dimmer. Fluorescent lamps can be dimmed via modified units, but only certain digital dimmers allow fluorescent lamps to be dimmed without any extra control gear.

A discharge lamp works by passing an electric current through a gas across two terminals. The initial 'arc' created gives a movement to the gas atoms of such magnitude that light is emitted. This process is called ionisation.

Although these lamps require a high surge of electricity to cause ionisation, once lit they are much more economical to run than tungsten-halogen lamps. Thus they are commonly used for industrial and street lighting, and when lamps remain on for long periods.

Colour-temperature factors apply differently from tungsten-halogen lamps. Whereas the latter emit light in all frequencies of the visible spectrum, the discharge lamp emits only a few specific frequencies. Although the light may appear white, under analysis it is apparent that this is due to the addition of individual wavelengths of light rather than a continuous wavelength. Discharge lamps are specified as having a colour temperature, but this is simply a (theoretical) approximation to a tungsten-halogen lamp. These lanterns are therefore specified as having a correlated colour temperature. Discharge lamps range in correlated colour temperature from below tungsten to above-noon daylight (see the table on p. 50). Colour filters can still be used with these discharge lamps, but will give slightly different results when compared with an incandescent source.

Because of the difficulties of dimming, the use of discharge lamps is restricted in the theatre. They are commonplace on the film set or in the television studio where dimming is less important. One very common lantern in film and television is the 2.5kW or 5kW HMI Fresnel. These can be fitted with controllable shutters which work like a Venetian blind to create a dimming effect. Unfortunately, these lanterns and their lamps are very expensive in comparison to conventional theatre fresnels, although these lanterns are often found in the larger theatres.

The CSI lamp is commonly used in followspots to give a very bright white light. To fade the lamp, either use an in-built mechanical douser or interrupt the beam by passing a 'fade-card' through it, located in a magazine of colours at the front of the lantern.

Slim-line fluorescent lighting is sometimes used to light the cyclorama, for a footlight, or for lighting concealed in the set, where its cool beam minimises hazards.

Low-voltage lighting equipment

In recent years the low-voltage lamp has become very common, particularly for shop display lighting and domestic task lighting. If a low-voltage lamp without a built-in transformer is run from the mains supply, a separate transformer is required to change the higher voltage of the mains supply to the lower voltage used by the lamp. The normal voltage used is 12 volts, and lamps with very small filaments are manufactured built in to dichroic reflectors (p. 70). The most common are the M-class family with 50mm diameter reflectors and these have proved excellent for display and directional lighting. Because the lamps are tiny, their lanterns also can also be very small. And because the dichroic reflector transmits much of the infra-red heat away from the beam, they are much cooler to work under. M-class lamps come in a variety of preset beam angles and power factors: from 8° to 60° and from 20 watts to 75 watts. The lamps are very efficient and produce a high light output for their size, as can be seen in examples in the table on the next page.

These lamps can be very useful in the theatre too, as they are highly efficient, have the colour temperature of a standard tungsten-halogen lamp, and they normally can be dimmed with conventional dimmers. As they are so small, they can often be concealed within a piece of scenery, or used discretely as a footlight. The normal theatre housing for these lamps is a mini-parcan, known as a 'birdie'. Like its big brother the parcan (p. 47), if you wish to change the power or the beam angle, simply change the lamp, checking that the power of the lamp is appropriate for the transformer that converts mains voltage to 12 volts.

How the equipment fits together

The next diagram shows how a theatre lighting system fits together. The lantern is rigged on a lighting bar and plugged into a socket on that bar. A lantern at floor level may be plugged into a floor-level socket called a 'dip'. The sockets are numbered. They extend via internal cabling or multicore cables to the

M-class lamp specifications

Thorn EMI Lightstream 50mm halogen dichroic 12v lamps.
Base GX5.3 Life 3000 hours

				Throw/Lux				
Type	Code	Watt	Angle	1m	2m	3m	4m	5m
M68	ESX	20	11	5000	1250	556	313	200
M94	BBF	20	24	1000	250	111	63	40
M71	FRB	35	8	9000	2250	1000	560	360
M70	FRA	35	18	3600	900	400	225	144
M81	FMW	35	38	970	243	108	61	39
M49	EXT	50	10	12000	3000	1333	750	180
M50	EXZ	50	21	3700	925	411	231	148
M58	EXN	50	38	1550	388	172	97	62
M80	FNV	50	60	700	175	78	44	28
M60	EYF	75	12	16000	4000	1778	1000	640
M82	EZZ	75	24	5500	1375	611	344	220
M61	EYC	75	38	2250	562	250	140	90

This table shows one manufacturer's range of M-class lamps. Each lamp is known by its type, e.g. M68, and the table shgows the range of beam angles and Wattages that are available, with lux levels.

dimmer unit. The lighting control desk and the main power supply are also connected to the dimmer. When the corresponding channel number on the lighting control desk is operated, the lantern will light up.

This 18-way system shows lanterns hardwired to the dimmers. A (digital) memory lighting desk connects to the (analogue) dimmers via a digital-to-analogue converter (demultiplex or demux unit).

A second diagram shows an alternative system, using a patch panel. Here the sockets on the lighting bar are not wired directly into the dimmers. Instead, the cables from these bars (and from all other plugging positions on stage) feed back to the patch panel which in turn is connected to the dimmer unit. As it is very unusual for more than 50 per cent of the dimmers to be in use for lighting at any one time, a patching system can be very cost-effective, as fewer dimmers and a smaller capacity control desk will be required. In the patching system if, for example at the end of a scene, a lantern is not needed again, it can be unpatched, freeing the dimmer for other lanterns to be connected. The main disadvantage is that the patched system has a smaller capacity and the occasional 'big state' or 'complex fade' sequence is impossible.

Lanterns hang from internally-wired bars or sit on stands; their cables feed either directly or via a patch panel to the (analogue) dimmers. The (analogue) manual control desk also plugs into the dimmers, as does the power supply for the whole system.

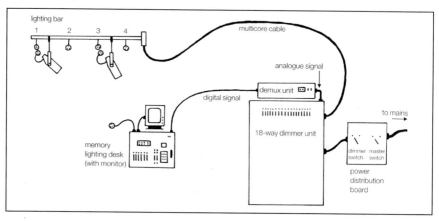

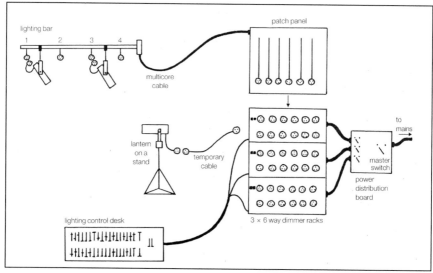

5 ANCILLIARY ITEMS: COLOUR AND SPECIAL EFFECTS

As well as the basic components of the theatre lighting system, there is the additional but essential equipment: gels to diffuse or colour a beam, equipment for special effects and making smoke effects, equipment for projecting images on stage, and specialist luminaries for creating light beam that move across the stage.

Diffusion gels

A diffusion gel or frost is a very useful way of adjusting the edge of a lantern's beam. For instance, for maximum light output with a profile lantern, the light must be focused to a hard beam edge. However, a slightly softer edge is usually required for overlapping profile beams. So, rather than defocus, fit a frost such as Rosco Supergel 119 Light Hamburg Frost to soften the edge. This is easier than defocusing and ensures all the edges of the beam are consistent.

Several frosts are available, ranging from those that give a slight diffusion to those that give a flood diffusion.

A 'silk' is a frost with a grain in the filter. This causes the beam to be 'stretched' in one direction and is useful for creatively lighting a corridor, or on a cyclorama where the beam is required to cover a large area.

Neutral density gels

Neutral density gels are 'grey' filters used mainly in photography, film and television to reduce light levels without altering colour. However, they are useful in the theatre to create dim stage lighting for they allow the running of a lantern at a high-intensity level (to maintain colour temperature) but with a low-intensity output. Neutral density gels come in various grades known as stops. The more stops, the darker the gel. Gel L209 reduces a lantern's intensity to 50 per cent; L210 to 25 per cent; and L211 to 12.5 per cent. Putting an L209 into a 1kw lantern effectively converts its intensity output to that of a 500 watt lantern. Therefore if a lantern is too powerful, neutral density gel can be used to 'stop down' its intensity to a more desirable level.

Coloured gels

Coloured gels are used to colour a lantern's beam. Although lighting gel is nowadays a polycarbonate-based medium, it retains the name given to it when it was made from pressed and coloured gelatine. Today there are various manufacturers of gel, each producing a different range of colours. Each gel is numbered, and this number is used for identification. The names listed in the manufacturers' sample or swatch books, e.g. 'salmon pink' and 'moonlight blue', are only used as a guide to the colour. Unfortunately, manufacturers do not have a common system for numbering gels. Most manufacturers produce different ranges of gel to cope with different heat emissions from different light sources. The most commonly used gels in the theatre are the high-temperature-resistant ones such as Rosco Supergel, or Lee Filters Polycarbonate range.

When selecting gel, always work under a light source of the correct colour temperature, and preferably hooked up to a dimmer so you can see how the colour is affected by dimming.

Deciding which colour gel to use is fraught with difficulties. To assist, the swatch books provided by the manufacturer not only show the colours of the gels, but also show the colours they are made up from displayed as a frequency spectrum graph. With red occurring at about 650 nanometres (see Chapter 2),

---

Swatch book graph samples

Three graphs taken from the Lee Filters swatch book to illustrate their relationship to the colour sample. The horizontal scale shows each colour wavelength, and the vertical scale shows the percentage of intensity of each frequency. Thus the graph shows how much of each individual colour is contained in the sample.

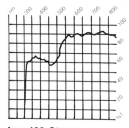

Lee 103 Straw
Approx. 65% blue,
80% green, 90% red.

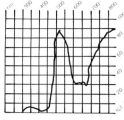

Lee 121 Leaf Green
Approx. 5% blue,
90% green, 30% red

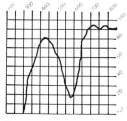

Lee 137 Lavender
Approx. 80% blue,
35% green, 80% red.

---

green at about 525 N, and blue at about 425 N, it is possible to see what other colours are present in addition to the dominant colour, and in what proportions.

Thus Lee 103, which is straw coloured, allows all the elements of the spectrum to pass, but only about 60 per cent blue. Lee 121, a leafy green, allows plenty of green to pass, 30 per cent of red and a negligible amount of blue. Lee 137, which is lavender, has good transmission of blue and red, but little of green.

You will see that the red end of each graph is rather distorted. This is because all gels let through infra-red light, which the actor will feel as heat.

The percentage of light transmitted by each gel is shown in the swatch as the transmission figure, e.g. Lee 103 Straw has a transmission of 81.6 per cent; 117 Steel Blue has 54.7 per cent; 119 Dark Blue has only 3.1 per cent. This helps when assessing the power of lamp required, as the lower the transmission percentage, the higher the power of lamp needed to obtain a strong colour on stage. Because the darkest tones let through such a small percentage of light, some extra measures must be taken to stop dark gels from

Sample colour selection	
Ten favourite gels for lighting plays. These are made by Lee Filters and Rosco	
Warms	
Lee 103	A gentle 'tobaccoey' straw, for candlelight, 'period' feel, interiors.
Rosco 04	A soft gold tint very subtle for warm daylight or interior and happiness.
Lee 154	A soft, feminine rose tint for daytime.
Lee 147	A deeper apricot tone for evening sun.
Neutrals	
Rosco 53	Softer and cooler than open white.
Rosco 351	In between warm and cool for a delicate tone.
Cools	
Lee 203	A cool, crisp blue for daytime and tension.
Lee 201	a deeper crisp blue for night-time faces.
Lee 117	Steel blue with a hint of green - good for moonlight and a 'period' feel.
Rosco 74	A dark blue for atmosphere and night.

malforming or burning up completely. Ventilating the gel by clipping it in a loop to the front of the lantern can help prevent this. Even medium-strong colour will fade over a period of time, so it may be necessary to replace some gels when a show is running for several performances.

When starting out as a lighting designer it is best to restrict yourself to a limited palette of colours. The basic palette of ten gels listed here is selected to light 'classic' plays, such as those by Shakespeare and Ibsen. You can of course add others as needed, and may like to experiment with bolder tones.

In addition to these gels, Rosco 119 Light Hamburg Frost, to soften profile beams, and Lee 210 Neutral Density, to check the intensity of over-powerful lanterns, would be useful additions. And of course do not forget the most useful gel of all, the one that comes free with every lantern purchased – open white!

Dichroics

A recent development in stage lighting has been the incorporation of dichroic glass to colour light. It is more efficient than polycarbonate as it filters to very precise bands of frequencies and gives purer, more vivid colours. Also, the glass is very strong and will not fade. Infra-red light in the form of heat from the lamp is reflected rather than allowed to pass through, so beams are much cooler than with polycarbonate gels. Dichroic material can also be used for lamp reflectors, allowing heat to pass out of the back of the reflector rather than be contained within the beam. Dichroics are most commonly used for lanterns with internal colour changers, e.g. moving lights (p. 77). Their expense and limited colour range has so far restricted their use in the theatre.

Colour-correction gels

Gels known as colour-correction gels have been manufactured to convert light of one colour temperature to another. Consisting mainly of cool blues and warm straws they have been primarily made for the film and television industry but are often used in the theatre to achieve tints of white light similar to sunlight conditions. The gels in the blue colour-correction family (Lee 218, 203, 202, and 201) change the colour temperature of the tungsten-halogen theatre lamp to the higher colour temperatures that are closer to daylight conditions. An open-white lantern will appear very warm in comparison to any of these gels. The gels in the straw colour family (Lee 223, 206, 205 and 204) are used in tungsten lamps to lower the colour temperature – useful in achieving a feeling of candlelight. Open white will appear cooler than any of these colours.

Colour changers

Often the number of lanterns on a rig can be reduced (and therefore the number of dimmers reduced too) if a lantern is fitted with a colour changer that offers a variety of colour choices. There are several types of automatic colour changer.

A motor-driven colour wheel containing five colours can be fitted to the front of a lantern and rotates to change the colour of the lantern. Another, more sophisticated type of colour changer is the semaphore, where up to six individual colour frames mounted in a magazine are dropped in front of the beam, allowing for subtractive colour mixing as well as the individual colours and open white.

MX Colour Wheel
CCT Lighting

The most versatile colour-change system is the colour scroller. This has a far greater range of colours than was possible with previous systems. Scrolls can house up to thirty-two colours: access to any one colour is possible within a split second. The scroll is controlled from a DMX control desk, which means that colour changes can be plotted as cues.

Semaphore
Strand Lighting

The colour scroll works like a roll of 35 mm camera film: it is a continuous strip of panes of colour. Motors drive the scroll backwards and forwards, stopping at the chosen colour position, as specified by the control desk.

The scroller has revolutionized lighting style where a lot of changing colour patterns are called for – such as in rock music and dance – and has drastically reduced the number of lanterns required on a rig. Although the motors in early scrollers were

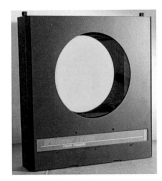

Whisper Scroller
Compulite/Stagetec

quite noisy, the current models are quiet enough for use in drama. This has opened up new design possibilities giving a 'live' colour change without a change of light texture as happens when cross fading from one gelled lantern to another.

It is interesting to note that the colour scroller is not really new. Coloured silks were scrolled around gaslights a hundred years ago to create colour change!

Casting shadows

Often shadow or shade is required as a contrast to even, unbroken light. Shadows can be cast on a screen or on stage by interrupting the light beam to achieve a broken light effect. This is done by placing some type of form between the lantern and the screen or stage. A KK wheel (a disc with slits in it that is rotated in front of a lantern) gives a flickering light effect like firelight. The effect works best using Fresnel or PC lanterns.

Shadows cast by trees or buildings can be recreated on stage using a device called a gobo. This is a small stainless steel plate with an abstract or figurative pattern cut into it. It is fitted into a profile lantern. The pattern is then projected onto the stage. There are many gobos available, from shapes of windows, logos and city skylines to abstract break-up lines and foliage. It is perhaps this latter group that is the most useful for providing convincing broken light on stage.

Gobo in a holder
DHA Lighting

Certain gobos, when used in conjunction with an animation disc (similar to a KK wheel) rotated through the beam, will give a moving visual effect. This is particularly good for effects such as running water. Because much light is lost by the combination of gobo and disc, it is best used with a high-powered profile. The most realistic images will be created when the unit is set out of focus.

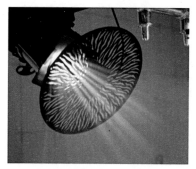

Gobos can also be rotated when fitted in to motorised gobo holder. The speed of which can be regulated from the control desk. Also, dichroic glass effects slides can

Animation Disk
DHA Lighting

also be projected as a gobo, rotated or used with an animation disc. These are capable of creating very complex and intricate coloured images, with very good colour rendition. The best known manufactures of these effects are Rosco and DHA.

Projectors

Images can be produced in slide format and projected onto surfaces to create scenery. Although the use of projection can at first seem useful, not only is it fraught with difficulties but it can cause restrictions as to how the play can be lit. It also can be expensive to obtain suitable projectors and high-quality slide material. You should also remember that projecting scenery creates a design style of its own and is not a solution to every design problem.

In addition, there can be problems of image distortion. Unless a slide is projected at right angles to the screen – and it is often not possible to place a projector in this position in the theatre – its image will be distorted. To combat this you need artwork that is counter-distorted. Either work out the angle of distortion using geometry or, when photographing material to make slides, take the photograph with the camera at an angle similar to the angle that the projector will be placed to the screen. When projected, the distorted image will correct itself on the screen.

For reflection of the brightest image, you should use proper projection-screen material, but anything opaque, including smoke, can be used. Projection-screen material comes in white, grey or black and there are different types for front or back projection. When back projecting, if proper screen material is not used, the projector lamp will be seen. The brightest images will only be obtained if the screen is placed at right angles to the line of sight. Unfortunately, there is often not enough space backstage to allow the throw necessary to achieve the correct image size. What is more, actors and backstage staff must be stopped from walking through the beam!

Although front projection gives the brightest image, it may be difficult to place the projector so that the actors do not walk through the beam and cast shadows on the screen. This can mean having to project at very acute angles to screen. Also, lanterns lighting the scene must be positioned with care so as not to bleach out the image.

However, if despite all this you still wish to use projected images, there are a number of possibilities for the theatre.

A Linnebach projector is a simple projector for creating unrealistic, abstract images. It consists of a painted slide placed before a lamp enclosed in a non-reflective housing. The sharpest images are achieved by using lamps with the smallest filament. A fresnel may be converted into a Linnebach projector by removing the lens and reflector and placing the slide in the colour frame runners.

An ordinary 35mm carousel-type projector is the standard instrument for projecting slides, but it is not very powerful for stage use unless there is no other competing light on stage. Specially adapted higher-powered units will cut through the competing light. Two projectors can be used with a dissolve unit which allows a fade from a slide in one projector to a slide in the other.

Various lenses can be fitted to projectors to give different image sizes, though a wide-angle zoom lens is the most versatile.

Sophisticated high-definition optical instruments for slide sizes up to 24 cm^2, such as Pani projectors are available, but these are very expensive. Beyond the budget of most theatres, they are mostly to be found in opera, television and the film studio.

The inexpensive overhead projector is surprisingly powerful and can be a

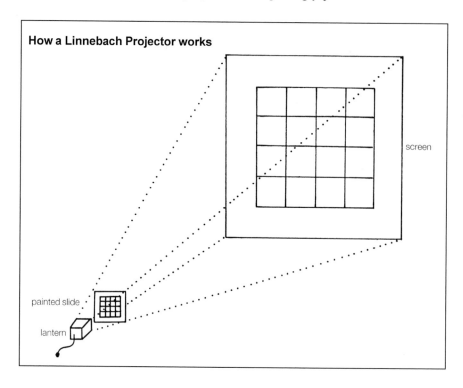

How a Linnebach Projector works

screen

painted slide

lantern

Ektapro 9000
Kodak

*2000W slide projector with image
scroller and slaved focusing*
Hardware Xenon

**Cadenza Effects
Projector**
Strand Lighting

BP4 Scenic Projector
Pani

useful addition to a theatre's stock. These projectors have a very high-quality image definition and slide material can be cheaply made up on acetate sheets using a photocopier. An overhead projector is useful for projecting titles on stage, for example as required in many of Brecht's plays.

Video Projection

Video projection is now a viable alternative for projecting still or moving images onto a stage backdrop. This medium opens up a whole new world of PC generated images which affords many exciting opportunities. However, the designer will find that the problem of gaining sufficient brightness from the image, when contrasted with the lighting needed to light the actors, remains a key factor.

Moving effects projectors

Lanterns such as the Strand Patt 252 or the Cadenza Effects Projector (pictured on page 59) can be fitted with moving effects discs. These are most convincing when two lanterns are used, one projected on top of the other and running at different (very slow) speeds. Disc effects include water and fire as well as various weather conditions.

Smoke

Smoke is used to create an atmosphere on stage, or sometimes to allow the beams of light to be seen. At times just a mist or fog is required; sometimes the 'architecture' of light beams shining through is the effect you want. Smoke

Peasouper dry ice machine
Le Maitre

1600 fluid smoke machine
Rosco

also acts as a diffuser, scattering and reflecting light. This reduces the intensity of light on stage and light levels may need to be raised as smoke is introduced. As the smoke clears, which it may do quite quickly in modern air-conditioned theatres, light levels may have to be adjusted down to avoid over lighting the scene.

Hydrosonic Haze Machine
Jem

Stage smoke effects can be produced by two different means: dry ice, and vaporizing a water-based glycol fluid. Dry ice is made of solidified CO_2. It forms a low-lying blanket of smoke across the stage that is created by lowering blocks of dry ice into boiling water using a machine such as a Pea Souper. Great care must be taken with dry ice as it is a very hazardous substance: always follow manufacturers' instructions to the letter.

Vaporizing fluid machines produce a fog that hangs in the air. These machines work by injecting a glycol fluid into a heater. The fluid is heated enough to produce smoke, but the lack of oxygen prevents combustion. Ducts carry the smoke out of the machine and onto the stage at controllable rates. Vaporizing fluid machines come in many different sizes, from hand-held battery units to those used by the fire brigade to simulate fire conditions! This type of machine can also be used, in conjunction with a cooling device called a 'Chiller' to produce a low-lying fog similar to that created by dry ice. Another version of this type of smoke generator is the hydrosonic haze machine. This produces a fine mist of smoke that is almost invisible until hit by light beams. It will hang in the air for a longer time, airflow through the theatre permitting.

Moving lights

One of the most spectacular develop-ments in lighting in the last thirty years has been the development of moving lights. Many stabbing light beams can now sweep across the stage in synchronized movements to give spectacular dancing light effects.

There are two types of unit. The first, such as the Vari*Lite, is a lantern fitted with a

MX10 moving mirror
Martin Professional

motorized yoke that automatically pans and tilts to preset positions recorded in the control desk. This can be done either when they are lit or in blackout. The motors can be noisy, although some models are quiet enough to be considered for use in drama.

Other features include dichroic colour changing to give a very wide palette of colour that can be changed many times a second; variable beam size for spot or flood lighting; and the use of a selection of built-in gobos. These features are controlled by a small microprocessor within the lantern, triggered by the main control desk.

The second type of lantern uses a motorized beam diverter mirror to move the light beam. There are several different manufacturers of this type of lantern, such as Clay Paky and Martin Professional. These units, like the Vari*Lite, also have dichroic colour changers and gobo options. The lantern sends its beam to a mirror that is panned and tilted by motors controlled from the control desk. These lanterns can move a light beam much quicker than the motorised yoke type.

Moving lights are principally found lighting discos, rock concerts and musicals, although they are sometimes used on stage for trick effects. In 'serious' drama there use is often confined to being a repositionable spotlight, or a recolourable area light. Rarely in this form of theatre do you see the beams move or change facility 'live'.

It is worth noting, however, that despite the sophistication of these luminaires, most will only move the light beam as pre-programmed by the designer. Although they may appear to follow the performer, it is in fact the performer that is following the light beam. A recent development has been an automated light called Autoilot, manufactured by Wybron. This light is linked by radio communication to the performer who wears a small transmitter. The light beam can "lock on" to the performer, and follow them around the stage automatically. This is particularly useful when the light is located in an inaccessible position, but the expense of the system precludes its use in most situations. The alternative, of course, is the human-powered followspot!

VL5 moving yoke
Vari-Lite.

6 THE DESIGN AND PRODUCTION PROCESS

The design and production of any play normally follows the same pattern, from selection of a text through to opening night. The lighting designer should be actively involved at all stages of the process, though in some instances he or she is given little say and will simply be asked to provide the lighting to suit the director's already-formulated ideas. Naturally this is less creative and less rewarding, but a good lighting designer needs to be able to adapt to any approach.

The team of people responsible for the visualization of the production, in other words for establishing the design concept, is known as the creative team. It consists of the director, set designer, costume designer (often these last two roles are combined), lighting designer and, if appropriate, sound designer and choreographer, but each member of the team carries his or her own personal 'toolbox' of insight, ability and enthusiasm. It is important that they can work in harmony, each accepting responsibility for the part they play in the realization of the entire concept.

I summarize below an example of a design and production process timetable. This is divided into three phases: preparation, development and realization. The figures in the left-hand column of the table refer to the length of time still to elapse before the opening night of a show. Of course, this is only a model and should be treated as such: every production has its differing needs, every director his or her different approach.

Other than being involved in preparing the design concept, a novice lighting designer may feel there is little to do early on in the production process. Then, all of a sudden, about ten days before opening, there is an enormous rush. In fact, once you have been asked to work on a show, there is always plenty to do to avoid a last-minute panic. In the early stages you need to read the script and get to understand the characters and how they develop during the play. You may need to do some research, for instance reading some critical studies of the playwright's work, to gain a fuller understanding of the text. Once the creative team has developed the design concept, its members will disperse to get on with their separate tasks, and the production can seem to go a little cold for the lighting designer. The director will be drawn away for casting and

Example of a production schedule

An example of a typical repertory theatre production schedule, as it applies to the lighting designer.

Preparing the design (-12 = weeks before opening)
- 12   script preparation
- 10   meeting with director
- 10   research
- 9   obtain groundplans of set/lighting plan of theatre, consider stock, budget, personnel
- 6   design meeting – exchange ideas, finalise concept
- 5   view set model and costume sketches

Developing the design in rehearsals
- 4   first reading with cast
- 4   start noting the blocking in rehearsals
- 3   draft cue synopsis
- 2   draft lighting plan and lantern schedule

Realising the design (- 7 = days before opening)
PRODUCTION WEEK
- 7   finalise cue synopsis and draw finished lighting plan to deliver to theatre for approval and copying
- 5   eve: cueing meeting to put all cues in prompt copy
- 4   am: rigging
          pm: rigging
          eve: rigging
- 3   am: focusing
          pm: focusing
          eve: plotting
- 2   am: technical rehearsal
          pm: technical rehearsal
          eve: dress rehearsal 1
- 1   am: work on stage
          pm: dress rehearsal 2
          eve: preview performance
  0   OPENING NIGHT/PRESS NIGHT
          followed by: production run and get-out

setting up rehearsals, the set designer will be busy constructing a set design model or 'model box', and the costume designer will be producing costume sketches. There may be little for the lighting designer to do other than attend early rehearsals and see the model box to start to get a feel of how the design concept is shaping up.

Once rehearsals are well advanced and the actors know where they will stand and move – in other words at quite a finished stage in rehearsal terms – the lighting designer can really set to work. There is still the frustration of having to hold back from designing the finished scheme until as late as possible in case of last-minute changes. This may be as late as a week before opening.

So the lighting designer is in a catch-22 situation. The later he leaves it to finalize his design, the more finished the production will be and, hopefully, the more chance there is of coming up with a lighting design that works. However, the design has to be ready sufficiently early for the equipment to be organized, rigged and focussed. The lights are normally hung just a few days before the show opens, in time for the technical and dress rehearsals. Even the most experienced lighting designer will be doing lots of tinkering in the last few days before opening, but you must remember that whereas a director can rejig actors' moves at the last minute, you may not have the time to reposition the lights.

Preparation

The first thing to do when asked to design the lighting for a play is to read the script. While interpretations may vary, the script is the fixed reference point for the whole production process. As you are reading, get a good sense of the storyline, how the main characters link to each other, how the plot develops and the play's key themes. Draw up a synopsis of the play scene by scene, detailing the incidents that occur in each scene. Note any points concerning the staging that are in the text. Some playwrights, notably Tennessee Williams, write detailed prefaces to each scene saying how they see the play being staged. Others write little or nothing. The text will also give you some clues to the lighting, for instance there may be references to the location of a scene, or its time of year or the hour of day.

The text will also suggest where cues are likely to come. Scene changes are obvious points where lights will change, but also look for a change in dynamics or a moment when an actor's entrance or exit might indicate a cue. Get a feel too for the size of the space needed for a scene. There may be six actors in a

A Flow Chart

An example of the opening of *A Midsummer Night's Dream*

Act/Scene	A1/S1	A1/S2
Synopsis / key moments	Theseus and Hippolyta plan to marry in four days. Celebrations ordered. Egeus complains to Theseus that his daughter Hermia wants to marry Lysander, not his chosen Demetrius. Egeus asks Theseus about marriage law. Demetrius wishes to marry Helena (Hermia's friend), but has since changed his mind. Hermia and Lysander plan to run away to marry. Helena decides to tell Demetrius in the hope he will think again.	etc
Location	Theseus Palace, Athens	
Time	Midsummer; the sun is setting, night draws in.	
Mood/atmos/ Emotion	Formal court; romantic; yet harsh decisions are taken.	
Cues	(Q1 Line 1) Theseus and Hippolyta enter; (Q2 L19) Egeus enters; (Q3 L127) Exeunt; (Q4 L225) exit Lysander; (Q5 L251) end of scene	
Composition -Positions	Key light sun from behind; soft fill; moonlight from side	
Composition -Intensity	Strong keys; overall state bright.	
Composition -Colour	Amber sun; watery moon; soft lavender fill.	
Composition -Texture	Even light, but can be localised for Q1 and Q4.	

small, claustrophobic room, or a single protagonist acting out his problems in the vast empty space of a windblown moor.

While you are reading, note the feelings that you have as these can act as a guide as to what the audience response will be, and that response can be underscored by your use of lighting. You may feel tension mounting or easing at a certain point; you may feel that there is a scary, chilly moment, or a moment for celebration. Does the mood early in the play prophecy the outcome, or does the mood of the play veer, perhaps from jollity and lightness, to inevitable doom and disaster?

Key words or phrases should occur to you during your reading, words that summarize the mood of the moment, or character personalities. Write them at the appropriate point in the synopsis. For example your key words may include evil, deceitful, power-hungry, cruel, jealous, innocence, impending doom, and so on.

These are words that are particularly useful to consider when trying to capture the mood of a moment in lighting terms. It may be that just a couple of these words will encapsulate what the whole play is about.

Next, select from the synopsis the most powerful dramatic moments. These in themselves will form a sort of pared-down synopsis, but one that summarizes the dramatic moments of the play rather than just the story. These are often the 'big moments' to consider that, once the lighting ideas for these are formulated, will drive the remainder of the design.

Gathering all this information may take you several readings of the text. Next, draw up a flow chart that collates all the information. The flow chart (see page 82) will be a combination of the scene-by-scene synopsis, with pointers to the lighting, notes on characterization and plot development, the key themes and moods of the play, its most dramatic moments and the emotional response provoked by the play at different points.

The flow chart also addresses the controllable parameters, pinpointing how the position of the lighting, its intensity, colour and texture can all be harnessed to give a visual interpretation. This analysis is a sort of 'lighting score' for the play and should be the basis for the finished lighting design.

Meeting the director and creative team

Roughly ten weeks before first night you will meet the director and the rest of the creative team and you should have your lighting flow chart ready by then. It is customary for the director to take the lead in outlining his or her interpretation of the style of the play, although occasionally the interpretation is devised by the creative team. Most often though it will be a two-way process, with the director bouncing ideas off the others and they reacting to the ideas, developing them and working them up into a visualization. At this early stage, most directors have plenty of ideas about how a play is to look but are unable to express those ideas in lighting terms. Part of your job as lighting designer is to help the director realize these ideas, to show him or her the potential that light has to shape a drama. It may take several meetings for the visual concept to emerge and, even then, the concept will be constantly reviewed right up until the last moment.

Developing ideas

Now you must develop these ideas and move towards representing them as a lighting scheme. You will already have done a lot of the spadework with your flow chart, but you will have to check that it tallies with the interpretation that has been put forward by the director and the others. You may need to do some more research, for example into the play's historical, social or political framework, or into its geographical location. Make a collection of any useful visual material you find during your research. It may help you to communicate your ideas to the rest of the team.

You cannot design the lighting without seeing the costume sketches and fabric samples. As well as becoming familiar with the style of the costumes, you need to know if the actors will be wearing hats as this may mean using a slightly lower angle to the lights to ensure that their eyes are lit. Similarly, the fabric samples will show you how reflective the materials to be used are and how they will respond to coloured light.

Have a good look at the cast as well. The range of tones of their skin is an important factor to be considered. Lighting a multiracial cast can be tricky due to the variety of skin tones. Note if any actor has deep-set eyes: like hats, eyebrows can prevent light from reaching the eyes.

Liaise with the set designer to see the model of the set – the model box – he is making. The model box will show the set, its structure, form, colour and texture and how the scene changes will work. From it you will see how much detail the set designer expects the lighting to provide: will the backdrop be lit or painted? Will light or structures define the stage area? Will there be suitable positions to hang the lights or will suspended scenery restrict the hanging positions? Will the rig need to be masked? Will cables need to be built into the set for the practicals, such as wall lights or skirting board plug sockets? How will the lighting be used to help along the scene changes? What will the pace of the fades be and how will this relate to the set and production style?

At this stage you also need to consider the equipment and range of technical possibilities that the theatre offers. Ask the production manager or chief electrician to supply you with a list of all the equipment available: lanterns, dimmers, control desk, power supply, rigging gear and so on. The chief will also supply a scale plan of the theatre with all the electrical facilities included. The scale used will normally be 1:25, or 1:50 for larger venues. Once the set has been finalized, ask the production manager for a copy of the set ground plan. Copy the plan of the lighting bars and electrical facilities onto tracing paper so it can be laid over the set ground plan to see how the two marry up.

Find out from the production manager what the budget is to hire or buy any extra equipment. You may be asked quite early on in the rehearsal stages to bid for part of the design budget. If you are prepared for this, you may be able to obtain money from the budget that might otherwise go to another department. The chief electrician will obtain quotes for any equipment that has to be hired or bought. He is the person responsible for submitting a budget request to the production manager and will negotiate the budget for the lighting on your behalf.

You also need to know from the chief electrician how many crew there will be to help with the lighting. There is no point planning to have four followspots if there is only enough staff for two to be used. One final constraint is that of time. How long has been allocated to rig, focus and plot the lighting, and how many people will there be to help with this? Are lanterns accessible from catwalks (quick) or from ladders or a tallescope (slow)? All these technical and organizational factors have their part to play in deciding on the lighting design.

Presenting lighting ideas

The final stage of the preparation phase is to present your lighting ideas to the rest of the creative team. From my experience, most directors like to have some visual reference material to look at as well as discussing ideas. A series of pictures might help to convey the ideas you have for a lighting design or, if the director has knowledge of art, a reference to a painting by an artist such as Caravaggio or Rembrandt can help conjure up the image you want.

You might use the model box or the flow chart. Although it is impractical to set up a real lighting rig to demonstrate an idea, torches or small, low-voltage lanterns (with halogen lamps so that they have the same colour temperature as the standard theatre lamps) are cheap and portable and can be effectively used with the model box to communicate your ideas. Use a gel swatch to colour the beam, and you will be able to present the full palette of colour available. You can also use the lights to illuminate fabric samples or skin.

The flow chart will show the development of your lighting composition and will hint at how the lighting pictures will link. Together, the model box and flow chart will show the rest of the team how the play will look.

Rehearsals

Now your research and planning is complete and the director and creative team are in agreement as to how the look of the play is developing. Read-throughs and rehearsals have started but you will be amazed at how much scope there still is for ideas to evolve further. The actors often bring tremendous new life to their characters, giving them a far greater emotional range and colour than can have been anticipated.

Blocking

With rehearsals under way you must start to plot out or 'block' the positions of the actors on stage and at what moments they move. This is easily done if you use a simple blocking notation, such as that used by stage management to note the actors' moves. You need to note every actor's moves on a mini set ground plan, and this must be referred back to the script (see page 89).

If you wish to free yourself from recording blocking at rehearsal time to simply concentrate on the acting, you might consider making a videotape of the rehearsals. It is best to set the video camera as high as possible to capture the actors' movements, and set the lens wide open to cover the whole stage.

Preparation of cue synopsis

By now you should be starting to imagine the lighting of the states and how the cues will work. If you have made a videotape of the rehearsals this will be invaluable in working out the timing of the cues away from the pressures of the rehearsal space, and you can use the VCR's second counter to work out fairly exact timings of the cues.

The result should be a cue synopsis that lists all the cues and states, explains where and how cues happen and what the states look like.

Noting actors' moves (blocking) – *A Midsummer Night's Dream*

① *Enter Theseus, Hippolyta, Philostrate and attendants*

THESEUS
(1) How fair Hippolyta, our nuptual hour draws apace. Four happy days bring in another moon – but O, methinks how slow this old moon wanes! She lingers... (19) ...triumph with revelling ②
Enter Egeus, Hermia, Lysander and Demetrius

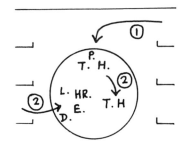

EGEUS
Happy be Theseus, our renowned Duke... (127) ...we will follow you. ③
Exeunt all but Lysander and Hermia

LYSANDER
How now, my love? Why is your cheek... (255) ...Demetrius dote on you.
Exit Lysander

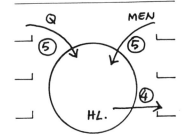

HELENA
How happy some......etc.
(251) ...and back again ④
Exit Helena. Enter Mechanicals ⑤

QUINCE
Is all our company here?... etc

Mini-groundplans are drawn. Characters' moves are then notated and cross-referenced to the text. This helps the lighting designer know how much of the stage area to light for each state, as well as establishing the cue points in the text.

Cue Synopsis – *A Midsummer Night's Dream*

Cue	Cue Point/Line	Cue Style	State description
1	Enter Theseus (1)	Fade up 3 sec	Blazing sunset backlight Theseus and Hippolyta, face lighting localising them on stage. Philostrate and attendants lit for secondary status. Cyclorama rich deep blue at top, with sunset at bottom. Moon projected onto cyc. Pinspot run up flats to look like columns.
2	Enter Egeus (19)	Add, 3 sec	Broaden stage picture.
3	Follow on (19)	X fade, 4 mins	Fade out sunset, fade in night.
4	Exit (127)	Subtract 10 sec	Close down stage to Lysander and Hermia.
5	Exit Lysander (225)	Subtract 10 sec	Close down to Helena, now full night, in sharp moonlit spot.
6	Exit Helena (252)	X fade, 7 sec	Similar to cue 1, but sunset key now from the side. Full stage.

Arrow plans

Arrow plans will help you get an idea of how your ideas can be converted into a realizable lighting scheme. Take some of the key moments in the play and draft sample lighting plans for each. You should avoid mentioning any specific lighting equipment, but instead should simply show the direction of the light required, the power needed, the spread of light and the desired colour effect. You might like to think of your arrow plans as the lighting designer's storyboard and you should do one for each state.

Arrow plans

Draw arrows on a groundplan of the set to show the direction of all the light sources for each state, noting: intensity, colour, area of focus and function.

A Midsummer Night's Dream – Act One Scene One.

1 key light – setting sun; rich golden intense full stage wash

2 sculpting mid-blue, full stage

3 sculpting mid-blue, full stage

4 dim face light – straw

5 dim face light – lilac

6 pins of light to make columns

7 cyclorama – top: dark blues; bottom pinks, golds, apricots

8 moon projection on cyc

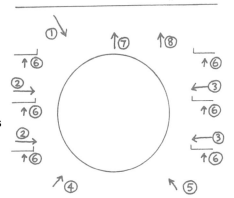

This plan shows the connection of the flow chart to the blocking displayed as a basic lighting plan. It is a stepping stone to the final lighting plan and lantern schedule. Arrow plans show ideas: they do not show which items of equipment will be used to realise them.

Drawing up the lighting plan

Now you must pull the arrow plans together into the proper lighting plan. Usually this will not happen until about a week before the technical rehearsal, so that you are familiar with all the blocking and with how the acting has evolved. But you must not leave it too late: there should still be time for the rig to be prepared and hung. You may also find that you need several attempts to get the lighting plan the way you want it.

With your cue synopsis and arrow plans to guide you, and your knowledge of how to position and choose the lanterns, decide which lanterns to use for each state and plot these in the correct positions on the lighting grid using a

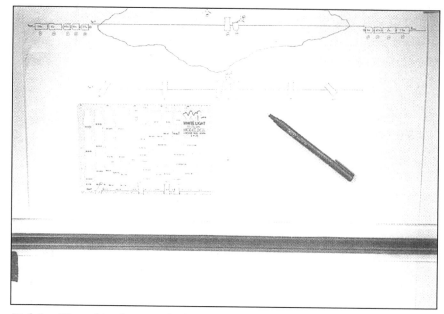

Lighting Plan: this photograph shows part of a lighting plan with lantern stencil and drawing pen

special scale stencil. (Chapter 7 deals with converting your ideas into a workable plan.)

Because the lighting plan is to act as a guide to the crew as to where to position the lanterns, it must be accurate, to scale and free of any unnecessary information that may confuse the crew.

Allocate a number to each lantern on the lighting plan. This number refers to the lantern schedule which shows what each type of lantern is, what colour it contains, to which dimmer it has been allocated, its function and where it is to be focused. When changes occur on the lighting plan, you must make sure that you update the lantern schedule. Finally, no later than seven days before opening, deliver a copy of the finished lighting plan and the lantern schedule to the chief electrician. This should allow plenty of time for the equipment to be prepared for rigging.

Realisation

During this last stage, you will be working closely with the theatre's team of electricians (a large theatre will have two or more full-time electricians while other crew are brought in if necessary) under the chief electrician and, perhaps, a deputy. The chief electrician's job is now to organize the lighting crew so that the lighting designer is freed from dealing with the rigging problems. As well as discussions the chief electrician will have had with you earlier about equipment and crewing levels, where possible he will also have read the script, will have seen the set design and should have seen a run of the play in rehearsal so that he is familiar with the whole project.

The chief will need to provide copies of the final plan and lantern schedule

Example of a colour call											
Colour call - *A Midsummer Night's Dream* - Act One, Scene One											
	L104	L117	L119	L147	L201	#13	#43	#48	#54	#70	#81
15° Profile (Cantata 11/26 180 x 180mm)		1									
1kW Fresnel (Starlette 180 x 180mm)										3	3
500W Fresnel (Minuette 120 x 120mm)					6						
650W PC (selecon 125 x 125mm)						5			5		
Par 64 (Thomas 250 x 250mm)	4										
1kW Ass. Fld. (AC1001 420 x 225mm)			3								
4 cell (Coda 235 x 215mm)	1			1			1	1			
L = Lee Filters, # = Rosco Supergel											

The colour call coordinates the variety and quantity of pieces of gel needed to be cut for every lantern size on the rig. The name of each lantern and its colour size is shown on the vertical scale and the colour number is shown on the horizontal scale.

Example of a lantern schedule *A Midsummer Night's Dream – Act One Scene 1*

No	Lantern	Circuit	Dimmer	Colour	Misc.	Focus/Function
1	Par64 CP62	8/01	48	L104		sunlight rays across SL
2	Par64 CP62	8/02	47	L104		sunlight rays across CL
3	Par64 CP62	8/03	46	L104		sunlight rays across CR
4	Par64 CP62	8/04	45	L104		sunlight rays across SR
5	650W PC	1/04	1	#13		front fill DC
6	650W PC	1/08	2	#54		front fill DC
7	650W PC	2/02	3	#13		front fill SR
8	650W PC	2/07	4	#54		front fill SR
9	650W PC	2/03	5	#13		front fill CS
10	650W PC	2/09	6	#54		front fill CS
11	650W PC	2/05	7	#13		front fill SL
12	650W PC	2/11	8	#54		front fill SL
13	650W PC	3/04	9	#13		front fill UC
14	650W PC	3/08	10	#54		front fill UC
15	1kW Fres	6/01	41	#70		across corridor, upstage
16	1kW Fres	4/01	40	#70		across corridor, centre
17	1kW Fres	2/01	39	#70		across corridor, downstage
18	1kW Fres	6/12	44	#81		across corridor, upstage
19	1kW Fres	4/12	43	#81		across corridor, centre
20	1kW Fres	2/12	42	#81		across corridor, downstage
21	500W Fres	F/03	49	L201	floor	pinspot uplight on flat
22	500W Fres	F/02	49	L201	floor	pinspot uplight on flat
23	500W Fres	F/01	49	L201	floor	pinspot uplight on flat
24	500W Fres	F/14	50	L201	floor	pinspot uplight on flat
25	500W Fres	F/13	50	L201	floor	pinspot uplight on flat
26	500W Fres	F/12	50	L201	floor	pinspot uplight on flat
27	1kW 15° prof	5/09	51	L201	G154	moon gobo on cyc
28	1kW Ass Fld	8/05	54	L119		top cyclorama
29	1kW Ass Fld	8/07	55	L119		top cyclorama
30	1kW Ass Fld	8/09	56	L119		top cyclorama
31a	500W 4 cell	F/09	57	L104	floor	bottom cyclorama
32a	500W 4 cell	F/09	57	L147	floor	bottom cyclorama
33a	500W 4 cell	F/09	57	#43	floor	bottom cyclorama
34a	500W 4 cell	F/09	57	#48	floor	bottom cyclorama

(SL = Stage Left, SR = Stage Right, DC = Down Centre, UC = Up Centre, CS = Centre Stage)

Each lantern on the lighting plan is given a full description in the Lantern Schedule. The information listed for each lantern includes: the type of lantern; the circuit number the lantern plugs into on the grid; the dimmer number the circuit is plugged into (or electronically patched to; any colour that is fitted; any miscellaneous information such as the use of gobos or floorstands; and notes as to its focus and function.

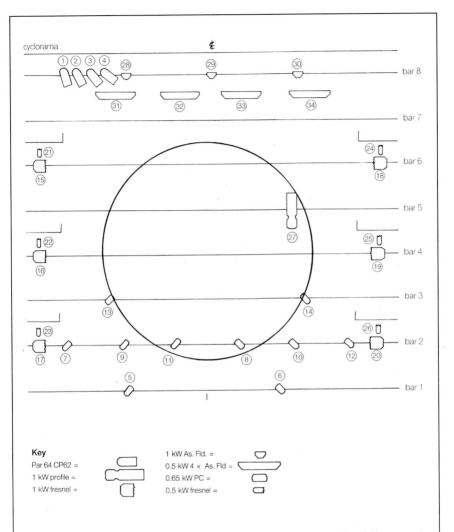

¢

bar 8

bar 7

bar 6

bar 5

bar 4

bar 3

bar 2

bar 1

Key

Par 64 CP62 =

1 kW profile =

1 kW fresnel =

1 kW As. Fld. =

0.5 kW 4 × As. Fld =

0.65 kW PC =

0.5 kW fresnel =

The set comprises of: a 5m (16ft 4in) diameter disc, rising from stage level (downstage) to 600mm (2ft) (upstage). discreet steps allow access at any point. The floor and masking is coloured in a neutral grey scrub, and the cyclorama is white.

Lighting bars are 5m (16ft 4in) above the stage floor.

Each lantern needed to create the design is drawn to scale on the plan and numbered for cross-referencing to the accompanying lantern schedule.

for each crew member. The lighting designer provides a list of all gels – the colour call – which shows the number of each colour required and the size to which it must be cut. All the lanterns, cable, colour and rigging equipment can now be prepared by the chief electrician to be ready for their time in the fit-up schedule.

Rigging

Rigging is the province of the chief electrician. During this stage the lighting crew work under his supervision to get all the lighting equipment correctly positioned, wired up and connected to the dimmers in accordance with the plan. All the gels and accessories such as gobos and barndoors must be correctly fitted, and finally everything must be 'flashed through', in other words checked that all is working properly.

Focusing

The next stage is called 'focusing' where each individual lantern is focussed to its correct position on stage. During focusing you will need quiet and blackout on stage in order to work efficiently. One member of the crew operates the control desk, while the lighting designer stands on stage to see the effect of each instrument. The focusers must work systematically along the lighting bars from a ladder, tallescope or catwalk, adjusting each lantern in turn. The beam must be centred at its correct location on stage, its width must be set and, if it is a profile lamp, its edge will have to be adjusted for hardness or softness. The beam may need shaping with shutters or barndoors. Once the lighting designer is happy with the focus of an instrument it is fully tightened, called 'locked off'. Some designers prefer to focus without any colour or diffusers in the lantern: it can be easier to see the beam this way. The gel is fitted once focussed.

The time needed to focus can be estimated by multiplying the time taken to focus one representative instrument by the number of instruments on the rig. Focussing will be quicker in a theatre with good access to the rig. This can be provided by catwalks or overhead lighting bridges. The geography of the set may make it slow to focus from a tallescope. It is important to try and keep to schedule with the focussing as any overrunning will encroach on the time the stage is available for other aspects of the production. Overrunning will not inspire confidence in the director or crew either.

Once the show has been focussed the chief electrician has to note the focus of every instrument on the rig so that if a lantern is accidentally moved, it can

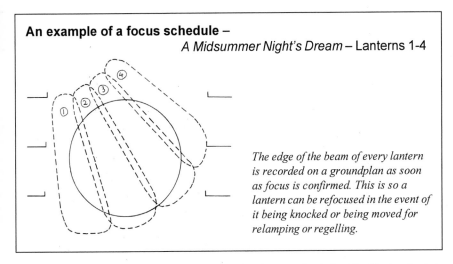

An example of a focus schedule –
A Midsummer Night's Dream – Lanterns 1-4

The edge of the beam of every lantern is recorded on a groundplan as soon as focus is confirmed. This is so a lantern can be refocused in the event of it being knocked or being moved for relamping or regelling.

be correctly focused again. This is called a focus schedule. Similarly, during the run, the chief electrician checks the rig daily for blown lamps, lanterns that have been knocked out of position, burned-out gel and so on.

Plotting

After focussing you are ready for plotting. This involves setting up the lighting for each of the states and recording them in the lighting desk. This is the first time that you can really see if the ideas you had on paper actually work in practice. There should still be time for some last-minute changes. These can be seen as a bonus, giving you the chance to be responsive to late changes in the production in a way that the other design disciplines cannot.

During plotting the director and set designer will be present, and a member of the stage management team will 'walk the moves'. At this stage your lighting may seem very raw: after all, there are no actors to fill the space and the whole thing is being seen out of context. You must make sure that there is plenty of time and calm for the plotting. The director will be expecting to see a scaled-up version of the ideas you talked about a month ago. However, this is your first attempt to 'mix the palette', so patience and good humour are often needed before you get into the swing of things.

Technical rehearsal

Once the show has been plotted, you are ready for the technical rehearsal. The play is run through moment by moment with the actors. All the crew and

An operator's cue sheet for a memory control desk

A Midsummer Night's Dream Desk – Arri Mirage

Cue No	Mem No	Playback	up/T	down/T	action/notes/cue point
0.5	-	-	-	7	fade houselights to B/O
F/O	0.7	A / B	-	7	fade preset to B/O
1	1	A / B	3	-	entrance of Theseus A1 S1
2	2	A / B	3	-	entrance of Egeus
F/O	3	C / D	1	-	move cyclorama sunset onto C / D
F/O	3.4	C / D	3.00	3.00	run sunset
F/O	3.7	A / B	-	1	remove cyclorama from A / B
4	4	A / B	-	10	close down to Hermia and Lysander
5	5	A / B	-	10	close down to Helena
6	6	A / B	7		X fade into A1 S1
F/O	6.5	C / D	7		clear C / D to B/O

Up and down times in minurtes and seconds.
F/O = Follow-on (i.e. run cue on from completion of previous).
B/O = Blackout.

This example shows cues running simultaneously in two separate playbacks. This allows a three minute sunset to run (on the C/D playback) independently of lighting changes for the actors (on the A/B playback).

actors will be busy sorting out their cues, so there will often be a quiet moment for the lighting designer to replot a state, to rethink a cue, or do a quick refocus. By the end of the technical rehearsal, all the cues and states and modifications will have been rerecorded in the lighting desk, and every member of the crew should understand all cueing operations.

Dress rehearsals

The two dress rehearsals give you the opportunity to assess the lighting under performance conditions, with each state seen in context and in real time with the actors' moves, the previous and following state. This is the first chance you will have to monitor the cues properly: check that each fade time is correct

Followspot cue sheet

Cue No.	Action In/Out	Colour	Beam Size	Pick up	Notes
5	FAST FADE IN	O/W	FULL BODY	D S L	
VISUAL CUE	SNAP OFF	—	—	—	AS ACTOR EXITS
15	SLOW FADE IN	L119	HALF BODY	U S R	
16	—	—	—	—	FADE OUT COLOUR OVER 5 SECS.
19	—	—	—	—	IRIS TO PIN-SPOT OVER 15 SECONDS
20	SNAP OFF	—	—	—	
26	SLOW FADE IN	L153	¼ BODY	C S	

This is an example of a plot sheet for a followspot operator.

Patching cue sheet

Dimmer	1	2	3	4	5	6	7	8	9	10	11	12	etc.
Top of Show	16	7	4 + 9	13	21	27	12	1 + 18	5	17	6	11	
After Cue 5				14						8			
After Cue 12				6									
After Cue 17	2	9	4					1					
After Cue 24		7	4 + 9					1 + 18					

This illustrates how to notate dimmer patching when allocation of lanterns to dimmers change during a show. Note the patch at the start of the show and repatches after a cue has been completed.

and that the instruction for the recall of each lighting state – the cue point – is set at the correct moment. There is normally enough time after the dress rehearsals for the last-minute refocusing that will be necessary if the director changes the actors' moves, and to make any last-minute replots on the lighting desk. Once the show is finalized, as a safeguard, copy the lighting desk disk and photocopy all the show paperwork. When the show finally opens, hopefully you will be able to sit back and enjoy it, although you will almost certainly still be taking notes to discuss with the director, stage manager and board operator later.

Computer aided production paperwork

Various computer-aided design systems have been developed in the last ten years or so to help the lighting designer produce a lighting plan and the associated paperwork. One common example is made by Rosco, who have produced a program called 'Lightwright'. This program will produce all the various paperwork reports such as lantern stock needs, colour call, and so on, once the rig information has been typed in. Any changes made to the rig will automatically be updated throughout the program. This helps keep all the crew abreast of things as the lighting evolves.

A more sophisticated program is Modelbox's Autolight. This program, as well as producing all your paperwork, will help with drawing the plan. Developed in conjunction with the AutoCAD program for set designers, the lighting designer can now access the stage's ground plan and the set ground plans on the computer screen. Lighting bars can be positioned on screen and instrument symbols placed on the plan. Sections of the set can be shown as well as the effect of a light beam from any given position and at any given angle.

You can also make a printout of the whole plan instead of drawing it by hand. As with Lightwright, this tool is particularly useful when you make any changes or update a rig. Changes can be keyed in and the updated plans can easily be printed. This system really comes into its own when touring; the rig can be quickly superimposed onto the stage ground plan of any venue. This makes it easy to see and make any necessary adjustment. However, for small to medium-sized shows, i.e. up to 200 lanterns, that do not tour, it is probably quicker to produce plans and paperwork by the traditional methods. While it is fair to say that these and the many other computer-aided design packages available today offer high-quality paperwork, their value to the lighting designer is far less than software packages are to set or sound designers.

7
CONVERTING IDEAS INTO A WORKABLE SCHEME

Having established a method for taking first ideas through the production process, the next stumbling block can be how to actually convert those ideas into a workable lighting scheme. There are certain techniques that have been developed to help with this.

Thinking of a lighting design in terms of lighting the states is relatively straightforward once you have decided where the cues occur in the play. You can simply plan the lighting for each state in turn. But this may require too many lanterns, dimmers and rigging positions. There is a lot to be said for notionally designing a show with unlimited equipment in mind: one can see how the ideal lighting design might work and, given that some lanterns may prove to be usable for several states, that ideal may actually be achievable.

Unfortunately, having unlimited equipment is unlikely to occur in practice and a lighting designer will have to make some compromises to achieve a workable design. It is the mark of a capable lighting designer that he or she can successfully deploy the available equipment.

There are two main methods for deploying lanterns in a compromise system to meet the requirements of a play: 'area breakdown' and 'key and blanket'.

Area Breakdown Lighting

The area breakdown, or actor's area, system of lighting greatly reduces the amount of equipment needed by demanding that the lanterns be multifunctional. This is achieved by, instead of viewing the play as a series of states, viewing it as a whole, but with its design requirements broken down into the following categories, each of which is relevant right through the play: lighting the actor's face; lighting the actor's space; lighting the actor's environment; and dressing the setting. If the designer addresses each of these requirements in turn, the result will be a lighting plan that encompasses the whole play.

Lighting the Actor's Face

Lighting the actor's face, which in practice also includes lighting the whole of the front of the body, is the most complicated of these four categories to realize. The best way to deal with lighting the actor's face is to use a technique that was first suggested in 1933 by the American designer and teacher Stanley McCandless in his book *A Method of Lighting the Stage*. It has since been advanced by many practitioners as being one of the best and most economical ways of achieving a natural style of face lighting over a large area of the stage.

The method used is to divide the acting space into zones about 2.5 metres (8 feet) wide, 2.5 metres (8 feet) deep and 2 metres (6½ feet) high. These figures are chosen because they represent an area that is a little larger than an actor's three-dimensional body space (see page 28). Any larger, and the area would be too broad and uncontrollable to light. One such area is then lit with sufficient lanterns to create the style required, and this is repeated in all other areas where this lighting style is required. You must remember though that to light the face and the front of the body on a proscenium-arch stage, lanterns must be positioned to the side or front of the actor. Lights that are positioned behind the actor will only illuminate the sides of his body or his hair.

For example, if your lighting style requires a natural daylight feel, you could light the face with two lanterns, one from either side of the actor at 45° to the vertical and 45° to the horizontal (see page 29) The plan for the downstage centre area of a stage 7.5 metres (24½ feet) square would look like the following diagram.

To cover the stage in this style of lighting, simply copy these positions across the whole stage area. The lanterns must then be focussed to light to just above head height (normally to 2 metres [6½ feet]) with a little excess to allow the beam to blend with the beams lighting the neighbouring areas (see page 104). There are many advantages to this method of lighting the actor's face. Actors can be individually highlighted if necessary by lowering the surrounding areas. It also has the advantage that the whole stage area is lit with an even consistent light, so that wherever the actor moves he will be part of a similar composition. Also, the beams hitting the actor from either side are approximately parallel, and this gives a sense of the light coming from single sources - in other words a natural lighting effect.

This area breakdown method of lighting is also very flexible. Individual areas of the stage can be dimmed, or lanterns from different sides can be coloured in different tones, for instance one side warm and the other cool, in classic lighting style.

When you have rigged or set up the lights for one cover over the whole of the acting area, then you can duplicate this rig with a second set - this is called 'double cover', and this gives an even greater range of lighting positions and colour. The two together provide a broad palette from which the lighting for the play can be mixed.

Lighting facilities to cater for area breakdown lighting have been built into most theatres in the last fifty years, with the result that many theatres have the necessary style of lighting rig permanently in place and focussed. All that is needed is for the lighting designer to choose the coloured gels he requires.

Once you have lit all the acting areas with appropriate face light, you can now consider the other three design requirements.

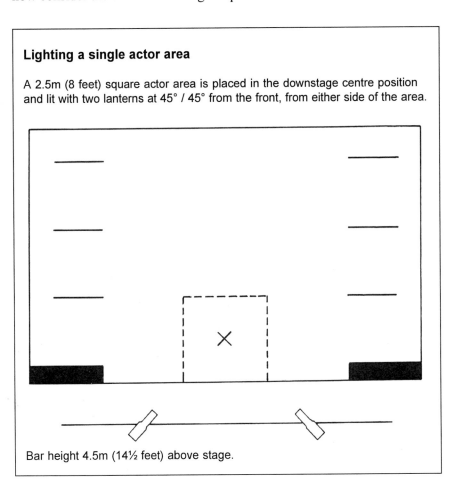

Lighting a single actor area

A 2.5m (8 feet) square actor area is placed in the downstage centre position and lit with two lanterns at 45° / 45° from the front, from either side of the area.

Bar height 4.5m (14½ feet) above stage.

Lighting the whole stage

A 7.5m (24½ feet) square stage divides into nine 2.5m (8 foot) actor areas. If possible rig lighting bars the same distance downstage of each rank of areas.

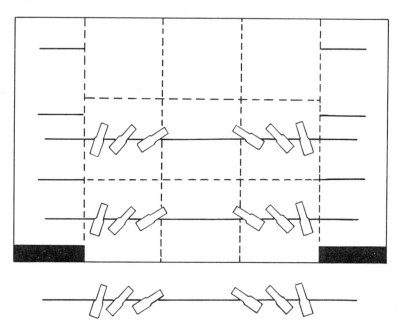

All lighting bars at 4.5 metres (14½ feet) above the stage

While it it possible to rig 45° / 45° lighting for the downstage centre, centre and upstage centre areas in this example, it is not possible to achieve this lighting style for the side stage areas. For these areas, each offstage lantern needs to be moved onstage to avoid lighting the proscenium arch or the masking as would be the case if they were placed in their true positions. Also, the onstage lanterns have been moved offstage along their bars as true rigging would superimpose lanterns on top of each other.

The result of this repositioning groups lanterns together rather than their being spaced equally. This gives the feeling of light rotating across the stage like rays of the sun, as if lit by a single source (from either side).

~This is a most useful lighting method as well as a variation when true 45° / 45° rigging positions are not possible.

Lighting the actor's space

The actor's space means the area of stage an actor or group of actors occupy at any given moment or in any scene. By using a single instrument or group of instruments to one side of or upstage of the actor, and powerful enough to cover the whole area of a scene, the actor's body shape will be 'dressed' and a sense that the space belongs to that actor will be created. When an actor is not highlighted with face lighting, he will be visible but will be of secondary importance to the principal. This technique is very useful for lighting extras in crowd scenes. Actor's space lighting could also define a room or equally well demonstrate a spatial or symbolic distance between actors.

Lighting the actor's environment

Lighting the actor's environment involves giving a sense of atmosphere, time or location to a scene. The lights may be positioned anywhere but they will be specially chosen or adapted so they add to the sense of atmosphere. Here you may use colour washes or higher-powered instruments to give a broad brushstroke of moody light across the stage. A single powerful source may be used to suggest sunlight or moonlight. Such a source may cast strong shadows which will be all the more convincing. Another option here for adding a sense of atmosphere is to use gobos. These give either abstract broken light or realistic light, e.g. giving the impression that a scene is set in a darkened room with light coming in from outside and casting the shadow of the window frame on the wall or floor.

Lights for the actor's environment can work in association with or as a substitute for actor's space lights.

Dressing the Setting

The final design requirement is to dress the setting, in other words to light the scenery, and the backcloth or cyclorama, and to add any special colours to enhance the setting as desired. The set may need specific lights to draw out certain details, colours or dimensions. Backcloths or cycloramas are often lit to suggest the time of day or to enhance a mood. This lighting can often be worked on the model box using a miniature lantern or torch coloured with the appropriate gel.

Before you start to match equipment to ideas and to position lanterns on a plan, write down the lighting you need for each of these four requirements. This will give you an overview and you can then start to think about which lanterns will be specials (lanterns with a single, dedicated function) and which may be multifunctional.

Breaking a text down into light

Example: *A Midsummer Night's Dream* performed end-stage in a small studio theatre.

Lighting equipment available: 60 lanterns; 24 **x** 10A dimmers fed by 100A supply; memory control desk. No access to the dimmers during the show for patching.

This is typical of the restrictions found in the smaller theatre. In this example, there is almost certainly sufficient power: 100A will give a brightest state of 24kW, plenty for a small theatre space. Sixty lanterns should be enough: so probably the greatest limiting factor to restrict the design will be the number of dimmers. (This example assumes it is not possible to supplement this number by hiring extra.)

When limitations of this nature occur, it is best to assess the overall design needs of a production rather than adopting the cue-by-cue approach.

What are the essential atmospheres to light? It could be argued that *A Midsummer Night's Dream* needs only the following (full stage) lighting states:

Palace in evening sun

A forest – human world

Palace at night

A forest – magical world

Additional 'specials' include a moon projection and Titania's Bower, and if a cyclorama is used this too will require light.

If two dimmer channels are allocated to the specials and two are allocated for the cyclorama, twenty channels will remain for the four main lighting states – an average of 12kW of power for each.

If this is insufficient power, or more 'specials' are desired, then further economies must be made. Perhaps the best economy is to use facelight common to more than one state – thus placing greater emphasis on actor space and environment lighting to create appropriate moods. By using one face lighting formula such as the McCandless style 'area cover system' for all the main states, the savings on power made over having four different sets of face lighting can give additional scope for crafted lighting environments.

If ten dimmers are allocated to face lighting, allowing each side of the face to be lit independently over three downstage and two upstage subdivisions of the stage (which also allows localized highlighting), then ten dimmer channels are left for environment lighting.

Further 'shared lighting' could still be employed. As all the play is set at night, a dark-blue atmospheric stage wash will almost certainly be required. If two dimmer channels are allocated to this, then eight are now left to differentiate the scenes.

Now, the needs of each particular state can be met. The palace at sunset only needs a powerful key light to complete the scene – one dimmer channel will suffice. And the palace at night will only need a moonlight key – again one channel. The human forest may need a full gobo-wash to give a realistic atmosphere. If two channels are allocated to this, then four are left for the magical world of Puck and the fairies – or 9.6kW of light.

This approach to lighting design may not respond to each moment in the play as well as a cue-by-cue approach, but it does offer a technique for when resources do not match demands. It also suggests what the most important aspects to light in a production are.

In many instances, an overview of a play in these terms will serve the lighting designer well even if there is greater equipment potential to realize ideas. Often a final design will pay respect to this overview approach with extra resources devoted to special moments or in making more sophisticated main states.

Key and Blanket Lighting

The 'key and blanket' method of lighting a stage, although now less common than McCandless's area breakdown system, actually predates it. It has its roots in the days when gas was used for stage lighting, and reached its peak in the 1930s and 1940s. It is still quite common today in the amateur theatre and is also used when a period feel is needed for the stage lighting. With this technique the stage is flooded with an unselective blanket of light into which highlights can be keyed. The blanket is provided by lighting the stage from above with rows of battens or floodlights grouped in different colours (often primaries). The result is a colour wash of light over the stage. Spots are then used as the keys to highlight the action. The key and blanket method requires less equipment than the area breakdown method, though it is a less sophisticated method of producing naturalistic-style lighting.

As well as being used for a period feel, key and blanket lighting can create a very moody effect. If the blanket provides sufficient visibility to create the atmosphere for the scene, extra key lanterns (for best effect use soft-edged followspots) can highlight the principal actors. And if the blanket of light is provided by one instrument, perhaps rigged high up and offstage, rather than by overhead floodlights, then you can keep the lighting over the acting area separate from the lighting on the set. A footlight (either a small spot, a floodlight or a striplight) offers another possible source for the blanket of light. It gives a particularly striking style of lighting and ensures that the actors' faces are always visible. If with key and blanket lighting you are considering using followspots for lighting the face, the need for face lights may be reduced. But you should remember that followspots impose a particular style to the lighting which may not be suitable for all plays.

Thus the area breakdown and key and blanket methods are good approaches to use when it is not possible to light a play with each state individually composed. They can also be used in conjunction with the state-by-state method, using the latter to light the main dramatic moments in a play and either the area breakdown or the key and blanket methods to provide a means of moving between the main dramatic highlights.

In-the-round lighting

The two methods of lighting a stage illustrated above are mainly geared towards the proscenium-arch theatre or end stage, which is an open-stage version of the proscenium-arch stage. Other stage types such as in-the-round stages, transverse stages or thrust stages need slightly different treatment because the audience views the action from more than one side. Because these stages usually have no backing such as scenery or a cyclorama, the lighting cannot really be as bold or adventurous as in the proscenium-arch theatre. Instead, the lighting designer can concentrate on atmosphere and texture. For these types of stage the area breakdown style of lighting can be adapted. Again, divide the acting area into 2.5 metres (8 feet) square zones and use three equally spaced lanterns with a 120° separation positioned above each area. For a fuller look, use four lanterns with a 90° separation.

If there is a lot of 'spill' from the lights into the eyes of the audience opposite, you may have to increase slightly the lanterns' vertical angle. Sometimes it is impossible to avoid lighting the audience, though in this type of theatre it is normally less important to keep the audience dark. Steep or vertical downlighting can be a useful way of colouring a floor or adding atmosphere. Gobos may of course be used for atmosphere too. Lanterns on opposite sides of an area are often paired to the same dimmer and may have similar colours. As with proscenium-arch theatres, double cover can give a wider range of tonal possibilities.

The key and blanket technique also has its uses with these types of stage, but is a less flexible technique. For instance, followspots are difficult to use effectively, while footlights can be problematic as they will result in the audience opposite them looking directly into the light.

Examples of in-the-round lighting techniques

Example 1 'Naturalistic' lighting

Having divided the stage into actor-area units, light each unit with four lanterns equally spaced at 90°.

This system works best with lanterns lighting the area from its corners, creating 45° light.

If lanterns are paired, then pair diagonals. If colouring lanterns, gel opposites in the same or similar colour.

The vertical angle of each lantern is best if between 45° and 60°.

actor zone

Example 2 A less realistic look.

For a less realistic look, or where economy prevails, three lanterns per area is usual.

Space the lanterns at 120°, again with a 45°-60° vertical angle.

There is no great advantage to pairing lanterns, or in using similar colours.

If using this method for, say, a moonlit night, set one lantern as a 'key' light and use the other two as 'fill' lights.

actor zone

These techniques are used wherever the audience partly or fully surrounds the acting area.

8 THREE CASE STUDIES

This chapter presents the case studies of three plays I have lit to show how a lighting design may be realised in actual terms. All three plays were similar in that they were each world premieres by leading playwrights, yet each required a completely different set of criteria. *When the Past is Still to Come* by Tom Kempinski was to be performed at a small fringe venue in London; *Mad Forest* by Caryl Churchill was commissioned by a major drama school and was performed in a studio theatre, then at the National Theatre of Romania in Bucharest, and later transferred to a West End proscenium-arch theatre; *The Clink* by Stephen Jeffreys was commissioned by Paines Plough Theatre Company, one of Britain's leading companies for the performance of new writing, and was to be a touring production, first in Britain, then in Holland and Belgium. So while all three plays were new works, the different locations in which they were to be performed added to the demands made on me in designing the lighting.

There are both difficulties and advantages to working on new plays rather than established texts. The advantage is that the writer is often present at rehearsals, giving the actors the benefit of his or her thinking about the text and the character development. This can greatly enrich everyone involved, including the lighting designer, and can help with some of the lighting design decisions. The disadvantage is that the author may still be developing the script as rehearsals progress, so the text, which with an established play is the one fixed point of reference for the creative team, is often subject to changes that can affect the design decisions.

The three plays illustrate different approaches to the construction of the lighting design: for *When the Past is Still to Come* I used key and blanket lighting; I composed the lighting for *Mad Forest* entirely from specials; and I based the lighting for *The Clink* largely on the McCandless acting area style.

When the Past is Still to Come

This play is an autobiographical account of Tom Kempinski's recent life as seen through his regular therapy sessions with his psychiatrist. The cast of two consists of the author and the psychiatrist. The whole play is set in the psychiatrist's consulting room and spans a period of about ten years. It is in thirty short scenes, each representing a session from the therapy.

The set design was based on Sigmund Freud's consulting room and consisted of minimal furniture and props on a circular stage about 6 metres (20 feet) in diameter. The problem for the director was that once the actors have entered they remain seated or lying down for virtually the whole play.

The lighting was to play a crucial part in the production. Although each scene had to be a realistic interpretation of a consulting room, the light had to be bright enough to help the audience focus on the very dense, detailed and intimate exchanges between the protagonists. It also had to emphasize the tension between them, as well as showing times of day and seasons of the year. Lights rarely changed during a scene, but the pace of the fade with which scenes started, as well as the delay between the last lines of dialogue and the fade at the end of a scene proved to be critical. These moments were very important for the realization of the whole play, and since the pace of the performance varied from night to night – something that was hardly surprising in a piece as intense as this – the desk operator, working a twelve-way manual desk, had to fully engage with the performance.

The lighting equipment available at the venue was minimal. Two 30amp supplies each fed a six-way dimmer rack. The dimmers were situated next to the desk operator, so patching was possible. There was a handful of 500 watt and 1kW lanterns and the lighting bars were positioned 4 metres (13 feet) above the stage.

The rig had to provide the realistic lighting for the consulting room so, following the key and blanket technique, I filled the stage with side and front/side lighting heavily stopped down by neutral density gel. This made it possible to run the lights at as high a level as possible to maintain their whiteness, while providing a soft, low-level blanket of light for the five key lights to bite into. I showed changes in the time of day by moving the key lights across the stage like the movement of the sun in the sky. In addition, by varying their height, I could indicate the changing seasons. I also used one special (a light on the on-stage telephone), a toplight to dress the whole set, and a 'boost' toplight for each actor's main position. There were fifteen lights on the rig. None of the lanterns were paired together on the same dimmer.

Mad Forest
The lives of ordinary people in Romania before, during and after the overthrow

of Nicolae Ceaucescu in December 1989 was the subject of Caryl Churchill's play *Mad Forest*. The play was commissioned early in 1990, when the events were still fresh in people's minds and when the world was hearing about the appalling conditions the Romanians were subjected to under Ceaucescu's dictatorship.

The creative team consisting of the writer, director, designer and myself were gathered together when the plans for the production were still very much in their infancy. The whole team was fortunate enough to visit Bucharest to do research, and the actors spent a week living with ordinary people there to get an idea of the impact the revolution had had on them. During our visit we had intensive workshop sessions with Romanian student actors who served not only as interpreters but also as sounding boards for ideas. To research a play in this detail is rare, but proved invaluable. The finished performance felt the most integrated and complete I have ever been involved with.

The play is in three acts. Act One concerns two typical yet contrasting families and the world they live in during the two years leading up to the revolution. Act Two documents some of the actual events of the revolution as they happened on the streets of Bucharest. Act Three shows the two families three months later, just before the Government elections. The families are now joined by marriage but facing many unresolved issues including guilt and tensions from their former lifestyle that affect their new-found freedom.

The scenes in the first and third acts are short and snappy: in Act One there are sixteen scenes, and in Act Three, eight. Several have little or no dialogue. Each of the scenes is linked by the sight of an English tourist walking across the stage reading from a Romanian/English phrase book. Act Two, by contrast, consists of a single scene with the actors almost completely static.

The set was the half-built, high-rise apartments of central Bucharest. A building site of breezeblocks and rubble dominated the open stage. The audience were seated crammed together on the breezeblocks.

The concept behind my lighting design was to create a harsh environment that underlined the fear, suspicion and uncertainly in which people lived. To achieve this I had to use specials throughout. In Act One, I lit the exterior scenes with a minimum of lighting – just one or two lanterns heavily stopped down with neutral density gel. This gave a low-level blanket of light to the acting area while I used a keylight (often stopped down too) to guide the audience towards the essential action.

The interior scenes of Act One had shadowy corners with the actors huddling together for warmth and security. Power cuts were common in Romania, so two scenes were only lit by candles. I used fluorescent light in the school room and hospital, while the practicals (lights on the set) had to reflect the style of fittings we found in Bucharest.

I made Act Three brighter. People were more relaxed after the revolution, but there was still tension, with politics being discussed at every opportunity and rumours abounding. The play ends with a wedding party disco. Guests are fighting over their beliefs while the Lambada is played to the accompaniment of crudely flashing lights coloured like the Romanian flag.

I deliberately made the rhythm of the lighting in Acts One and Three reflect the brutality of the times. Houselights were snapped randomly on and off during the scene-change links involving the English tourist, and although I included timed fades at the end of scenes, all the scenes opened with the states snapped in, to make the audience feel rather unsettled.

Act Two, set during the revolution, takes place in a vast underground bunker. Here I used Mercury Vapour industrial lamps in converted Strand Patt. 502s, to give a very eastern European feel. The audience was lit as brightly, if not brighter than the actors, to draw them in as bystanders to the action.

The lighting control was limited to a small memory desk and twenty-four 10 amp dimmers, but fortunately I had no need to abandon any lighting design ideas for either technical or financial reasons. The cue sequences were very complex so I needed a second operator in charge of the non-dims (those devices that do not operate via a dimmer) and a complex rolling patch. There was a low grid 4 metres (13 feet) above the stage in the studio theatre which worked well for this production, allowing me to have lanterns at low angles slashing light across the stage and contrasting with narrow-beam toplights as highlights. This meant that there was often a great deal of light spill into the audience, though normally at low intensity levels.

The Clink

This play is set in the political world of the court of Elizabeth I. While the country waits for the elderly, childless queen to die, her ministers snipe and manoeuvre for power, hindered by the fact that she still has to name her successor. The story is seen through the eyes of the court jester who runs the risk of losing his head for treason through his telling of political jokes.

The play moves from location to location across London: the royal court, under London Bridge, a conference chamber, the Queen's chamber, the Clink prison. The set design consisted of a raked stage and backing wall made of slats and cut out in the shape of a map of Britain. There was a central upstage high-level platform where Queen Elizabeth sat throughout the play. The costumes were in period style and metallic music punctuated much of the action, underscoring the dialogue. Much of the music developed during improvisation in rehearsal and was performed both by musicians and the cast.

The director wanted simple lighting. Cues were to be used to denote the end of a scene or a change of dynamic or emphasis. The states were to provide realistic lighting bright enough for dense, lengthy scenes to take place, but sometimes heightened and quite stark to emphasize the tension of the action and the ugliness of the characters and situations. Although there were many comic moments, the overall mood was pessimistic.

Because this play was to go on tour, the lighting rig had to be fairly small. I divided the whole stage into nine areas, following the acting area lighting technique, so one area could be picked out while the lighting in others closed down, or so that separate actor groupings could be highlighted.

I finally settled on a colour palette of open white and Lee 202 – a brittle steel blue. I placed the principal instruments with the blue gels either side of the stage at a high angle to give a very sculptured look to the actors. This texture was filled with open white from the front of the stage and from above. I then added a second layer of key lights, again using side lights with Lee 202 gels, but this time coming in at head height and using narrow focus to create very intense side stabs of light. I alternated these from either side so that an actor walking down the centre line of the stage would be hit by alternating beams from either side. This heightened the contrast of each beam and created a dynamic visual addition to the palette. I also used footlighting a great deal to add to the sense of intrigue, as well as many special highlights where necessary.

I had one idea early on which was to link each scene with a single lighting state to symbolize the continuing flow of the River Thames. I achieved this with an animation disc coloured in dirty blues, yellows and brown used with a 2kW 30° profile lantern from a high backlight position. The aim was to suggest not only the river, but also the endless detritus that the river carried through the city and, by analogy, the political intrigue that runs throughout the play.

FURTHER READING

I believe these are the six most useful books written on lighting, essential for every serious book shelf:

Bergmann, Gosta. Lighting in the Theatre, *(Stockholm: Almqvist & Wiksell,1977).*

Gregory, R.L. Eye and Brain. The Psychology of Seeing, *(London: Weidenfeld & Nicolson, 1969).*

Hays, David. Light on the Subject, *(New York: Limelight, 1989).*

Keller, Max. Light Fantastic. The Art and Design of Stage Lighting *(Munich, London and New York: Prestel, 1999).*

Palmer, Richard. The Lighting Art, *(New York: Prentice Hall, 1985).*

Pilbrow, Richard. Stage Lighting Design: The Art - The Craft - The Life *(3rd ed), (London: Nick Hern Books, 1997).*

Other recommended reading referred to in the book:

Health and Safety Executive. Electricity at Work Regulations, *H.M.S.O., 1989*

McCandless, Stanley. A Method of Lighting the Stage, *3rd ed., New York:* Theater Arts, 1947.

The main organisations that represent the interests of lighting practitioners in the UK are:

The Association of British Theatre Technicians (ABTT)
www.abtt.org.uk

The Association of Lighting Designers (ALD)
www.ald.org.uk

The Professional Lighting and Sound Association (PLASA)
www.plasa.org

INDEX

ENTERTAINMENT TECHNOLOGY PRESS

FREE SUBSCRIPTION SERVICE

Keeping Up To Date with

Stage Lighting for Theatre Designers

Entertainment Technology titles are continually up-dated, and all major changes and additions are listed in date order in the relevant dedicated area of the publisher's website. Simply go to the front page of www.etnow.com and click on the BOOKS button. From there you can locate the title and be connected through to the latest information and services related to the publication.

The author of the title welcomes comments and suggestions about the book and can be contacted by email at: stage.lighting@etnow.com

Titles Published by Entertainment Technology Press

ABC of Theatre Jargon *Francis Reid* **£9.95**
This glossary of theatrical terminology explains the common words and phrases that are used in normal conversation between actors, directors, designers, technicians and managers.

Aluminium Structures in the Entertainment Industry *Peter Hind* **£24.95**
Aluminium Structures in the Entertainment Industry aims to educate the reader in all aspects of the design and safe usage of temporary and permanent aluminium structures specific to the entertainment industry – such as roof structures, PA towers, temporary staging, etc.

The Exeter Theatre Fire *David Anderson* **£24.95**
This title is a fascinating insight into the events that led up to the disaster at the Theatre Royal, Exeter, on the night of September 5th 1887. The book details what went wrong, and the lessons that were learned from the event.

Hearing the Light *Francis Reid* **£24.95**
This highly enjoyable memoir delves deeply into the theatricality of the industry. The author's almost fanatical interest in opera, his formative period as lighting designer at Glyndebourne and his experiences as a theatre administrator, writer and teacher make for a broad and unique background.

Introduction to Rigging in the Entertainment Industry *Chris Higgs* **£24.95**
An Introduction to Rigging in the Entertainment Industry is a practical guide to rigging techniques and practices and also thoroughly covers safety issues and discusses the implications of working within recommended guidelines and regulations.

Focus on Lighting Technology *Richard Cadena* **£17.95**
This concise work unravels the mechanics behind modern performance lighting and appeals to designers and technicians alike. Packed with clear, easy-to-read diagrams, the book provides excellent explanations behind the technology of performance lighting.

Lighting for Roméo and Juliette *John Offord* **£26.95**
John Offord describes the making of the production from the lighting designer's viewpoint - taking the story through from the point where director Jürgen Flimm made his decision not to use scenery or sets and simply employ the expertise of Patrick Woodroffe.

Lighting Systems for TV Studios *Nick Mobsby* **£35.00**
Lighting Systems for TV Studios is the first book written specifically on the subject and is set to become the 'standard' resource work for the sector.

Lighting Techniques for Theatre-in-the-Round *Jackie Staines*, **£24.95**
Lighting Techniques for Theatre-in-the-Round is a unique reference source for those working on lighting design for theatre-in-the-round for the first time.

Lighting the Stage *Francis Reid* **£14.95**
Lighting the Stage discusses the human relationships involved in lighting design – both between people, and between these people and technology. The book is written from a highly personal viewpoint and its 'thinking aloud' approach is one that Francis Reid has used in his writings over the past 30 years.

Practical Guide to Health and Safety in the Entertainment Industry
Marco van Beek **£14.95**
This book is designed to provide a practical approach to Health and Safety within the Live Entertainment and Event industry. It gives industry-pertinent examples, and seeks to break down the myths surrounding Health and Safety.

Production Management *Joe Aveline* **£17.95**
Joe Aveline's book is an in-depth guide to the role of the Production Manager, and includes real-life practical examples and 'Aveline's Fables' – anecdotes of his experiences with real messages behind them.

Sixty Years of Light Work *Fred Bentham* **£26.95**
This title is an autobiography of one of the great names behind the development of modern stage lighting equipment and techniques.

Sound for the Stage *Patrick Finelli* **£24.95**
Patrick Finelli's thorough manual covering all aspects of live and recorded sound for performance is a complete training course for anyone interested in working in the field of stage sound, and is a must for any student of sound.

Stage Lighting for Theatre Designers *Nigel Morgan* **£17.95**
An updated second edition of this popular book for students of theatre design outlining all the techniques of stage lighting design.

Technical Marketing Techniques *David Brooks, Andy Collier, Steve Norman* **£24.95**
Technical Marketing is a novel concept, recently defined and elaborated by the authors of this book, with business-to-business companies competing in fast developing technical product sectors.

Theatre Engineering and Stage Machinery *Toshiro Ogawa* **£30.00**
Theatre Engineering and Stage Machinery is a unique reference work covering every aspect of theatrical machinery and stage technology in global terms.

Model National Standard Conditions *ABTT/DSA/LGLA* **£20.00**
These *Model National Standard Conditions* covers operational matters and complement *The Technical Standards for Places of Entertainment*, which describes the physical requirements for building and maintaining entertainment premises.

Technical Standards for Places of Entertainment *ABTT/DSA* **£30.00**
Technical Standards for Places of Entertainment details the necessary physical standards required for entertainment venues.

for full details go to etbooks.co.uk